Y2K GOLD RUSH

"How few like Daniel, have God and gold together."
—Bishop Henry Montague Villiers

Y2K
GOLD RUSH

WADE B. COOK

GOLD LEAF PRESS

Copyright © 1999 Wade B. Cook

Library of Congress Cataloging-in-Publication Data
Cook, Wade.
    Y2K gold rush/Wade B. Cook.
    p. cm.
    ISBN: 1-882723-36-8
    1. Gold--United States--Purchasing. 2. Investing--United
    States. I. Title. II. Title: Year two thousand gold rush.
HG295.U6C66 1998
332.63--dc 21   98-31994
                                                             CIP

Source Code: Y2KGR98

Production: Brent Magarrell
Book Designer: Judy Burkhalter
Cover Designer: Marina McDonagh
Production Technicians: Jeff Allen, Cynthia Fliege, Scott McRae
Photo Credits: pp 37-44—Zachary A. Cherry
Proofing/Editing: Robin Anderson, Kathryn Drinkard, Laurie-Jo Jones, Bethany McVannel
Contributors: Merelynn Bates, Paula Carmen, Sam Hemenway, Karen Larsen, Grace McLinn, Jim Powell, Kathy Smock, Juliana Warner

Published by Gold Leaf Press
A subsidiary of Wade Cook Financial Corporation
A public company, ticker symbol: WADE
14675 Interurban Avenue South
Seattle, Washington 98168-4664
1-800-706-8657
206-901-3100 (fax)

Printed in the United States of America
10 9 8 7 6 5 4 3 2 1

To Uncle Bob,

You are pure gold

CONTENTS

PREFACE

The end of one millennium and the beginning of a new one should engender wonderful, happy and even reverent feelings. After all, we're still alive. God is alive and well. The sun continues to rise and set each day. The stock market is about 200 years old and still offers wondrous investment opportunities. Real estate prices are up. Babies are still being born, and man, with his unquenchable thirst for knowledge, continues to explore medicine, space, communication, technology and relationships. What a grand and wondrous time we live in!

However you view things, though, the front page of the newspaper and the sirens on the six o'clock news continue to peddle the negative aspects of our future. Recently, the CEO of Ford said (and I'm paraphrasing), "It will lead to a recession if everyone keeps waving their arms and panicking."

The latest bogeyman lurking in the shadows is the Y2K issue. I surely don't need to rehash all aspects of the problem here. It will be sufficient to say that the year 2000 will be interpreted by many computers as the year 1900 or some other double-digit zero year.

You don't have to search very far to find major levels of mass hysteria. Supposedly, planes will fall from the skies, hospital and credit card records will disappear, equipment will run amok, and banks will fail. The list is almost endless.

Is there a problem? Yes. Is it as bad as everyone thinks? Not likely. It will be a short-lived runny nose, not a fatal cancer. Consider the following:

1. Most companies have already fixed their computer problems.

2. The government is slow, but its systems will get fixed. And so what if the government shuts down for a while? I think it would be a nice change.

3. Hundreds and thousands of tests simulating potential situations have been conducted and will continue to be conducted. The test records for fixing this problem are incredible.

4. This is America. Remember "Yankee ingenuity?" "Necessity is the mother of invention." We invent solutions to solve our problems. And we do it quickly.

In a recent edition of Bloomberg magazine, Michael Bloomberg says, "This is, of course, a happy time for calamity hysterics and the people who make money feeding others' fears ... Y2K is not a descrete thing, an event tied to a single event on a single date, but a series of events striking months before and months after the millennial moment."

It's almost uncanny. Last week I taught a new seminar on gold, Y2K, and their connection. I said that the only people I see hyping the Y2K problem are the fear mongers with something to sell or something to gain directly from an increase in the problem. I also stated that it would be a hiccup and a much-overrated "crisis" than most presently imagine. Then I got home and read the statement by Mr. Bloomberg. It's amazing. He also said, "The bug won't be Armageddon. It'll be more like the flu; you sneeze and sniffle, and you get over it" and, "So a lot of these fears are just not realistic, a point ably demonstrated by the Securities Industry Association, which recently ran tests involving thousands of simulated

New York Stock Exchange trades with nary a glimmer of dooms-day. But if you're a consultant, you can sell the idea to a company that perhaps it has a problem. They key word is perhaps."

For me, there is a silver lining to all this. I really like gold investing from several points of view. I have been teaching a seminar on gold for 14 years. This seminar, to a certain extent, has fallen on deaf ears. Most of my students think real estate is exciting, or stocks are where it's at. Gold just seems boring. Not to me. I'm so glad people are finally taking a new interest in gold. Ironically, much of this new found interest is promoted on and around the internet. Whatever the reason, it's good to have people taking an interest in gold.

You can't depreciate it or collect rent on it. It's the ultimate hassle-free investment. It's portable. It feels good. It's versatile. More importantly though, it's a factor in calculating the rate of inflation. It's in demand by millions worldwide, and has been a medium of exchange for thousands of years. In short, it's worthwhile to own.

Now, more than ever, a certain portion of your assets should be in gold. Hyperinflation or serious deflation are bigger threats than the Y2K bugaboo. The probability of economic distress as a nation or community, and the potential of a downturn in your own personal economy, makes investment in gold a positive hedge against these problems.

Surely we want to buy and accumulate before the need arises. We want to buy wisely to maximize our profits. We want to own the "right stuff" and have it properly stored. We need to avoid the pitfalls of wrong purchase strategies.

We need to understand the benefits of ownership and the solutions gold ownership offers to the visceral fear that is perpetuated by today's fear mongers.

The time is right for you to start acquiring gold.

Publisher's note: Many chapters of this book are adapted from live seminars and lectures by Wade Cook. While this style may be hard to follow at times, the free flow of ideas lends energy and vitality to the learning process. For a complete list of Wade Cook's books or his speaking schedule, call 1-800-872-7411.

If one should give me a dish of sand, and tell me there were particles of iron in it, I might look for them with my eyes, and search for them with my clumsy fingers, and be unable to detect them; but let me take a magnet and sweep through it, and it draws to itself the almost invisible particles by the mere power of attraction. The unthankful heart, like my finger in the sand, discovers no mercies; but let the thankful heart sweep through the day, and as the magnet finds the iron, so it will find in every hour, some heavenly blessings, only the iron in God's sand is gold!

—Henry Ward Beecher

ACKNOWLEDGMENTS

If Dawna Foucht had not brought the current Y2K hysteria and the accompanying demand for gold to my attention, this book would not have been written. Thank you, Dawna.

Many people helped put on paper my seminars, my strategies, my thoughts. Thank you to Brent Magarrell, Bethany McVannel, Marina McDonagh, Cynthia Fliege, and Judy Burkhalter.

Thanks to my sweetheart, Laura, for helping me collect and categorize our gold and for being the best darn wife a guy could have. I hope her computer chips don't go haywire between 12-31-99 and 01-01-00.

Other Titles By Wade B. Cook

101 Ways To Buy Real Estate Without Cash
Cook's Book On Creative Real Estate
How To Pick Up Foreclosures
Real Estate For Real People
Real Estate Money Machine

Bear Market Baloney
Stock Market Miracles
Wall Street Money Machine

Blueprints For Success, Volume 1
Brilliant Deductions
Wealth 101

A+
Business Buy The Bible
Don't Set Goals (The Old Way)
Wade Cook's Power Quotes, Volume 1

THE Y2K
FACTOR

There are negative issues that continue to come up in the minds of Americans everywhere. It seems that we as a people have a tendency to gravitate towards the negative aspect of any situation. I don't know where this comes from. This country is built on the backs of positive thinking, forward looking people—people who get out and put their shoulder to the wheel and make things happen. But still there continues to be a tendency to dwell on the negative and have it taint our thinking process and sometimes consume our lives.

Specifically today there is an issue that is a foreseeable and potentially real problem: the year 2000, or the "Y2K" computer problem. I think to a certain extent it is going to be taken care of in many, many ways.

Now, it's pretty amazing that, although it's been in the newspaper almost every day, there are still some people who do not understand what "Y2K" means. So, I'll quickly give an explanation of this simple phrase.

Y2K DEFINED

When referring to Y2K (sometimes YTK), the 'Y' stands for year, the '2' is simply the number 2, and the 'K' represents kilo, or 1,000. Taken together "2K" means 2000, or 2 millennia. Put them together and you have the Year 2000.

The Year 2000 problem is specifically associated with computers—mainframe computers, internet computers, banking computers, airline computers, embedded chips in electrical power systems, nuclear power plants, and even cars and toasters. Any computer that needs to keep track of a date after the year A.D. 2000 is a potential candidate for the Y2K problem.

By the way, a quick little point—a lot of people think that the millennium changes on January 1st of the year 2000. This is not true. The millennium change will be January 1st of the year 2001. The year 2000 is the last year of this millennium, and the millennium changeover will be in the year A.D. 2001.

Now let's go back and talk about this computer problem. Historically computer BIOS (hardware) and software only use a two-digit number to represent the year. December 25, 1998 is generally stored as 12/25/98.

There are concerns that when we hit January 1st, 2000 (01/01/00), computers won't know the difference between 1900 and A.D. 2000. This is a real problem. It really exists and it can cause a lot of havoc here in the United States and worldwide.

Now, this is a book about gold and you've got to be asking yourself, "What is he talking about? What does this have to do with gold? Why should I buy gold for this problem?" Well, those are the issues we are going to address.

One of the reasons gold has come to the forefront at the current time is because all over the country the use of the internet has become so pervasive. Millions of people log on every day. The latest numbers I read stated that over 80 million people worldwide are hooked up to the internet and this number is growing at a rate of up to 10% per month! Recently, negative comments and information have been spread through the internet saying that the whole economy is going to collapse. Supposedly, the sky is going to fall in the year 2000.

Why would I doubt the powers of the internet to sell stuff that nobody else can sell? Why would I doubt that when I see internet stocks trading at 900 times earnings, and even 9,000 times earnings? I've invested in three or four internet companies that have just gone through the roof. They're trading at thousands of times earnings, which means you're going to pay thousands of dollars for stock to get at one dollar worth of earnings. But they're saying that in the year 2003, the year 2004, when this company finally makes money, the stock will be worth it then. Well, I don't believe that the stock market is that forgiving. I think people should be really, really careful about buying into the hype of internet stocks. But, the point is, the internet has the ability to sell people on an idea, and create a hysteria that I think is unfounded.

Several years ago when we started getting into the 1990s, people realized, "When we come up on the year 2000, and the date switches past December 31st, there may be airplanes up in the air flying that won't know where to land because it's the wrong century." Everything's just going to go haywire. It's like the Twilight Zone, you know? "You've now entered the Twilight Zone." And that creates a lot of scary stuff.

By the way, I see people now worrying about whether the little computer chip in their toasters is going to work right! "This toast is going to be in there for 100 years." How ludicrous.

So, because we have become a computer chip laden society, and our economy, from banking and finance to credit cards, use computers, there is a big worry. Companies have come into existence that didn't exist even ten years ago, specifically to develop software programs to solve this problem. They go from company to company, computer system to computer system, dealing with this Y2K problem. Good!

But some say it won't be enough. Therefore, these fear mongers say, you'd better get to the number one store of value that has historically been the best place to have your money in times of crisis, and that is gold.

You go into bookstores now and all their books on gold are sold out. Coin dealers now are doing very, very well selling gold coins. Why? Because there is a certain hysteria that has been created and there are a lot of people who have started buying gold due to this hysteria.

I've been teaching and preaching about gold for years and sometimes I've felt like the pews were empty and the few people who showed up didn't really want to hear about gold because there was so much excitement in real estate investing and so many thrills in stock market investing. The stock market has been so wild the last couple of months, even the last year, that it is better than going to Las Vegas. It's just been a thrill a minute!

There is so much excitement that people have ignored my cry for the last 14 years. The coins that you will see in this book were in my original bag of coins that I started using in my seminars 12 to 14 years ago. Some of these are now a bit tarnished because they've been in there so long.

I have been teaching and preaching gold: Buy gold! Buy gold! Buy gold! Now all of a sudden everybody is taking an interest in it; it looks like my new gold book is going to be an overnight success. Why? Because there's interest in it that I didn't create. I've been trying to drum up responses for gold for a long time. I've got another best-selling book out in the marketplace called *Wealth 101*. There's a great section in *Wealth 101* on gold investing—one of the best in the whole country. But to a large extent, my entreaties to get people to buy gold, my dedication to teaching people good principles about gold have previously been ignored. Now all of a sudden, there's a big excitement. Now all of a sudden, everybody wants to buy it. Why? Because of the internet and the Y2K problem.

Is there still going to be a problem in the year 2000? Is the problem in the year 2000 different in America than in other countries around the world? What about some countries that rely on computers to run their banking systems, but do not have the sophisticated new software they need to correct the problems with their internal computers? Is there a problem? The answer is yes—but nowhere near the problem some have created or imagined.

THE Y2K PROBLEM

I believe in Yankee ingenuity. I believe that we are the "fix it" country. We can muster up forces like you would not believe. We were caught with our pants down at Pearl Harbor in 1941, but within months we mobilized a whole workforce of trained workers to build airplanes and get them up in the skies. We can do amazing things in this country when we put our minds to it. We are a country that lives by the motto "Necessity is the mother of invention." When there's a need, we rise to the occasion like nobody else.

My point is that I don't think the Y2K problem is going to be as pervasive and devastating as some people on the internet want it to be, or make it seem. As a matter of fact, I'm going to make a pretty bold statement. I know there are going to be a few exceptions to what I'm saying, so if you find an exception, please don't write me letters and please don't send me copies of internet articles. I have probably seen, in the last year and a half, 100 to 140 news reports and magazine articles about the Y2K problem. But I have not yet seen one report from anybody who is predicting that the sky is falling or that there is going to be a huge catastrophe who did not have something for sale. Let me say this again: integral to the article, or to the company putting out the report about the catastrophe that's going to happen to your company, or your business, or the whole government infrastructure, or the whole country, there is always somebody trying to sell a newsletter or computer software service that you can hire at such and such a fee to come in and fix your problems. The only people I see who are telling us there's going to be a huge negative problem are people that have something to gain by it being a huge negative problem.

Now, I know there may be some exceptions. There may be someone pure of mind who doesn't have anything for sale. By the way, I sell seminars. I sell stock market seminars. But I don't think it's going to be that big of a problem. I'm not telling people to come to my stock market seminars to learn how to invest in companies that have been started up and totally dedicated to the Y2K problem, because I just think it's a nonstarter. I think it's a fad right now that will quickly go away. I personally am afraid of investing in some of these companies simply because if I invest in them, what's going to happen after the year 2000 and 2001? If these companies don't have other products or services for sale, they're not going to have any business.

So what do I think is really going to happen? I think that about 80% of American companies, according to the last report I read (and it was a very comprehensive report) have already taken care of the problem. Of the other 20% that haven't taken care of the problem, many are not date sensitive. For instance, take a concrete company laying road repairs and pouring foundations. If their computer has to be adjusted within three or four months after January 1st of the year 2000, so be it.

Now banks, airlines, and companies like that are the ones that are the most date sensitive. Most of them have taken care of the problem, at least to a certain extent. They realize the potential dangers and loss of revenues, and are being proactive about it.

What about the U.S. government? I wish I could say that we have a bunch of really, really sharp, smart people back in Washington, D.C. running this country. But, if there is any grouping of people that know how to bungle stuff, it is government agencies.

Now, most of you are going to realize that when it comes to being right or left on the political structure, I'm about 800 yards to the right of Attila the Hun. I mean, I'm way over there. I would love the government to be curtailed and stopped for a while. It needs to get back to the Constitution and only do what it is licensed to do by the Constitution. We would all be a lot better off.

This last summer, the summer of 1998, a huge test was conducted. Some companies did not even know they were part of the test until just a few days before it started. I think 160 or 180 companies were involved. We are talking about multi-billion-dollar companies and a few hundred million dollar companies. They picked a day and ran a test to see what all their computers would do as they switched over to the year 2000. The results were nothing short of spectacular! They were remarkable results! Apart from a few little glitches, and a few paper trail type problems that didn't happen correctly, nothing of a substantial nature went awry. Most of these companies made the transfer over with very few problems.

By the way, they have scheduled three more tests. I think the first one is going to be with 1,000 companies in every state in the country, and the next one will be with up to 5,000 in May or June of the year 1999. They keep doing these tests to literally see what happens when these companies' computers switch over to the year 2000 using all the old Y2K infested software.

We have a problem out there, but we've already dealt with that problem to a certain extent. Software programs have been written to search out and correct the date problem. New software programs have come into existence in the last five to seven years that almost any company can utilize, which will help them pass through the millennium. They are ready to go.

I'm sorry guys, I know there's a lot of people reading right now that want me to sit here and bad mouth and say that everything is going to fall apart. I just don't believe that to be true.

By the way, the people that are going to criticize me for having a bit of a Pollyanna attitude towards the year 2000 issue are the ones that are trying to scare you and sell you stuff. I'm trying to enliven you and lift you up and say, "Guys, this is the time for us to get going."

OTHER PROBLEMS

There are other problems related to Y2K that are of a minor nature.

September 9, 1999 is going to be a problem. A lot of programmers built into their computer software programs safety valves that can potentially cause computers to crash on September 9, 1999. These safety valves, which are stored as 9999, are sometimes called an end-of-file marker. They tell the computer it has reached the end of a chain of data and the software responds by going on to the appropriate action. Most computers store this date as 9/9/99, see the problem there? Since most everybody knows about this in the computer industry, to a large degree, the problem has already been taken care of.

Also, the year 2000 is a leap year. Most computers calculate and account for leap years every four years. When the original calendar was made, they put an extra day in February every four years that most of us are familiar with. The end of a millennium, however, has to make a minor adjustment for having a leap year.

THE CONSPIRACY THEORY

There are people that think the whole Y2K issue is a conspiracy initiated by the federal government. They believe that the federal government literally wants everything to come to a grinding halt. My goodness! The federal government bungles everything. Can you imagine what they'd do if they attempted to take over the whole world by shutting down every computer in other countries and using that as a way to take over? I hear this kind of stuff everywhere. Where does this kind of negative, conspiracy theory stuff come from? There are just so many negative people that I think you ought to be very, very careful to whom you're listening. If there is going to be a problem in the year 2000, it's not going to be one created by the federal government. It is going to be one that you have created.

Everybody just calm down and keep your lips shut. Like my mom used to say, "If you can't say anything nice, don't say anything at all." Well, if you can't say anything nice about this country, don't bad-mouth it! Most people don't know what they're talking about anyway. This is a great economy. I love this country. I see this country and the economy here as strong as ever.

Recently there was huge talk about the stock market going down. I just could not believe it. Everywhere I turned, this negative comment was repeated. I have a subscription internet service called Wealth Information Network™ (W.I.N.™). Anybody can log on the internet under wadecook.com and read the reports that I have made on this subject.

THE BOTTOM LINE

The topic is Y2K, and there is a problem. But I think it is mitigated by a lot of things. There is a problem in us, in our attitude and there is a problem with the rest of the world. I believe we are resilient, not just as Americans, but as a people.

This problem is not going to go away for a few years. It is a real problem. And it will take a while for our economy and others to come back.

You've got to learn. You've got to be educated. That's my point. If there's going to be a fiscal downturn, it will not be in anybody's economy except your own. It comes down to your own attitude and what you know. Now, how does gold play into this? How does the stock market play into this? Can we use this experience right now to maybe clean house? Can we use this experience right now to say, "I," meaning you and me, "need to get better educated." And, how do I do things a little bit better?

What I'd like to do is start with gold and then go through different ways of investing in gold, then move onto different angles of the stock market, and other angles of investing that will help you keep your own head out of the gutter. Not to be an ostrich, but just get it where it needs to be.

Along with the possibility of catastrophe and calamity also comes the opportunity for advancement and profit. Are you ready for the opportunity?

But he knoweth the way that I take: when he hath tried me, I shall come forth as gold.

Job 23:10

A vain man's motto is: "Win gold and wear it;" a gener-
ous, "Win gold and share it;" a miser's, "Win gold and
hoard it;" a profligate's, "Win gold and spend it;" a
broker's, "Win gold and lend it;" a wise man's, "Win gold
and use it."

—Author Unknown

 # GOLD AS A HEDGE

For thousands of years gold has been a marketable item, a store of value. Before paper currency, gold and silver were cast and coined, and this was one of the early methods of standardization in many countries. Archaeologists have long collected these coins for decorative and museum purposes. Gold has been used as jewelry for centuries. Recently gold has come to be recognized as a form of currency, and as a reserve for paper currency.

In the latter part of the 19th century, as a result of the Industrial Revolution, there was a widespread international adoption of what is called the "gold standard." The countries that adopted this standard had seen an enormous increase in the production of goods and a widened base of world trade. Principally, the objectives of the gold standard were to simplify international business and financial transactions, ensure stability in foreign exchange rates, and stabilize domestic monetary rates. By having a single standard of international validity and stability these goals could be accomplished.

Great Britain was the first country to convert to the gold standard in 1816 and most other countries, including the United States, followed suit by 1900. It was the economic crisis of 1929 and the following depression that signaled the end of the gold standard.

Some dramatic things happened toward the end of the 1920s. The years 1929 through 1933 were sad times for our country. I hope and pray it will never happen again. I know most of you find it unimaginable that the government could control our lives to the extent of literally demanding our gold. It's not as sad that the government took advantage of its citizens, but that we as citizens allowed it to happen. In the movies, you have seen pictures of Fort Knox and all the bullion bars there. Where did all that come from? It came from Americans turning in their money.

Our government minted gold coins for many, many years. Other gold was stored at Fort Knox. Then, in 1929 and up to 1932, the government called in all the gold. Americans were told by the Federal Government that they could no longer own gold—gold dust, gold coins—all of these had to be brought in. The government repossessed gold currency from private citizens. Everyone had to bring in their gold, although they were allowed to keep some jewelry. Everyone thought they were getting a good deal because the government paid $20 an ounce for the gold when it had been trading for $16 an ounce. But then, after the government had taken all the gold back, in 1931 and 1932 they arbitrarily set the price of gold at $35 an ounce. Franklin D. Roosevelt, in 1933, took the U.S. off the full gold standard and adopted the "modified gold bullion standard." Gold was still used in defining the value of the dollar and the dollar was set at 1/35 of an ounce of gold. Gold was taken in at a $16 value and was then raised to $35—thereby cutting your buying power by one half. From 1931 to 1934 nearly all world governments abandoned the gold standard. In part, this was motivated by the belief that devaluing currency against foreign exchange rates would stimulate exports. This advantage was slowly offset as other countries abandoned the gold standard as well.

I hope we learn lessons from this. We need to be the protectors of our interests. We need to elect people that will protect them for us. We seem to elect people we believe will go to Washington, D.C. to protect our interests. However, many of those elected officials get there and start taking things away from us. They start taking our assets through taxation or through other means. They are not acting in our best interests for the most part. So be very, very careful whom you elect to these government offices.

The period of time from the 1930s, actually the end of the 1920s, clear up through 1986 saw no more gold coins minted in America. That was a sad time. All of the gold was in a storehouse in Fort Knox and a few other places. As we became more of a global society, and expanded business with various countries around the world, we got economically caught up in those countries' affairs. We realized that a lot of things needed to change. There was a major shift in foreign policy beginning in 1969 and ending in 1973.

In one of my real estate books (*Real Estate Money Machine*) I use this quote by George Washington. When he left the White House he was asked the question, "How will this country survive?" He answered, "We need to avoid costly entanglements." This advice, given back in the 1700s, is still applicable today. We, as a country, need to avoid costly international entanglements.

After the Second World War, world economies weren't doing that well. The United States had poured a lot of money into the war to help in the effort, but there was a great deal of pressure for these countries to pay back the investment America had made in them. There began the switch in 1968 and 1969 to what now is called a monetary policy, where the dollar is backed up by the full faith and pledge of the United States Government. Silver or gold, no longer backed the actual paper currency. Slowly then, the Federal Government was able to begin selling off those stockpiled gold bars.

It was 1975 when gold was diminished further due to the government selling its holdings on the open market, making gold more of a commodity than a standard in the international monetary system. It was in 1978 that Congress officially removed the U.S., on an international basis, from the gold standard.

We've not been on the gold standard since that time. By the way, look at what has happened to the currencies around the world with all the fluctuations. We really should get back on the gold standard, but I don't see that happening. I hear talk about it every now and then. I see currencies around the world that are still on the gold or silver standard that are much more stable than ours.

In 1986, the government began minting gold again. With the United States hundreds of billions of dollars in debt, the government said, each time we sell this gold at whatever premium, part of the profit is going toward reducing the national debt. What a joke. Pennies against dollars to reduce the federal debt. But that was how they got this thing through. We'll take all this gold sitting there in Fort Knox, melt it down, make it into coins, sell them, and take part of the money to pay down the federal debt. What it gave them, by the way, was a way to raise billions upon billions of dollars that they could spend on all kinds of socialistic programs.

By the way, since we went off the gold standard from 1969 to 1973, look at what has happened to the value of the U.S. dollar. Ten thousand dollars is now worth right around $3,000 in buying power—hard buying power. That is what happens when the paper currency is not tied to any hard metal backing it up. We are now living in a country that exists in a world on a complete monetary policy. Is it going to go away? No. This country has stood the test of time—it will be around for quite a while. Will it go through problems? Yes. Will it go through economic problems? Yes. Will there be dips and spikes and peaks? Yes. There will be all kinds of interesting things in our stock market, in our economy and in our business dealings around the world. This point is interesting because our currency will float by the level (or amounts) of money the Fed places into the market.

Now, let's go back between 1969 and 1973. Can I give you a comparison of what happened? If you were to look at a chart of the U.S. dollar against all the currencies in the world, at least the major ones, you will see that from time to time the dollar is strong or weak against the Japanese yen, or against the German mark. Those are the two major comparisons—the Japanese yen and the German mark. Today the United States, Japan, and Germany are the three major economic super powers in the world. Have you noticed that nobody ever compares our dollar to the Swiss franc? And why is that?

Let me give you an example. I don't have exact numbers, I'm just paraphrasing now, but I hope you get the point. If you were to see a chart of the United States dollar and the Swiss franc, you would see a sad comparison. Let's say that you put $10,000 actual cash money into a savings account in the United States about 25 to 28 years ago. Then you put another $10,000 into a Swiss savings account. What has happened to the value of U.S. dollars compared to Swiss francs and what are the values of your accounts today? Skip ahead 25 to 28 years, and let's find out the buying power of both of your accounts. The U.S. account would be worth something like $3,900 and the buying power of the Swiss account is right around $9,990. I mean it is almost a whole $10,000. Now, why is that?

Again, I am trying to put this in perspective so you can really feel what is happening in this country. Why the strength of the Swiss franc? Because the Swiss franc, by its constitution, is backed up by gold. As a matter of fact, it is backed up with a 200% gold clause. For every paper Swiss franc on the street, there is 200% of gold in reserve.

We, in the U.S., have sold off our gold. We have switched off of a gold standard into a new policy called a monetary policy. Our dollar is based on what everybody thinks it is worth, or whatever the government tells us it is worth. You can't take $20 or $50 bills any more and convert them into silver or gold. There is no such ability. We have gone totally away from that.

From time to time you will hear people, from major government players on down the line, say we need to get back to the gold standard. I think it would create such a weird situation in the world for us to do so, but I also believe it would be a good idea. It may take five or ten years to do that, but we do not have enough votes in Congress. We do not have any political leaders I know of in power today that would even vote for us going back on the gold standard, and yet it would be one of the most safe and sane things we could do in this crazy world.

One of the reasons I believe in investing in gold is because we, as a country, have gone off the gold standard. We have become a pure monetary country. However, just because we have gone off the gold standard does not mean that you, as an individual, need to go off the gold standard. You can still own gold. You can have gold to back up your retirement. You can have gold to back up hard times in your life, or hard times in our country's life. Let me say it again—just because the country goes off gold does not mean that you need to go off gold.

We own gold because it will always be a good store of value—just as it has been for thousands upon thousands of years.

The law of thy mouth is better unto me than thousands of gold and silver.

Psalms 119:72

Gold, like the sun, which melts wax but hardens clay,
expands great shoulders and contracts bad hearts.
—Antoine Rivarol

A LOOK AT GOLD

One of my favorite books is **Business Buy The Bible**. At the beginning of that book, I talked about the age old quest by many people to find a way to manufacture gold. Alchemy and all of its derivative discoveries have been a boom to mankind. We have all benefited. I'll use a part of that same chapter here.

For thousands of years, men set out to create or make gold. It was an alchemist's dream. Thousands of various mixtures and processes have been tried. Gold, for centuries, even millennia, has been a store of wealth, a medium of exchange. It continues to be so today. The commercial uses of gold from industrial use to jewelry, from printing and art to dentistry are legion.

Isn't it ironic that men have so diligently tried to find a way to make gold, but if successful (while helpful) it drives the price down? Their newfound riches dissipate under the avalanche of an abundant gold supply. Part of the reason gold is so valuable is because of the difficulty of finding, mining, and processing it to a usable point.

Is the endeavor worth it? I am one who believes in, and lives by, a serendipity philosophy. The many happy and joyous discoveries I've made while looking for, or attempting something, have made my life not only interesting, but enjoyable and fulfilling. Likewise, all alchemists' attempts were not in vain. Some spurred our pharmaceutical industry. Some gave us more durable metals like steel and aluminum. Others helped us harvest bigger and better crops.

In our current study of gold, I'll deal primarily with American gold highlights, which by itself limits the complete industrial origins, usage and worldwide context, but also is more interesting to us as Americans.

Gold has been discovered in virtually all of the original colonies. When the early Americans arrived they did not need to originate needs for gold—those needs already existed.

As politics matured, one political division was between people who wanted gold as the standard and those who wanted silver. Toward the middle of the 1800s much discussion and political debate occurred. Americans were sharply divided. The main point is that the paper currency increased its value because of a metal—at least to a certain extent. Paper was convertible. Trade it in for gold or silver.

All this dramatically changed. Let's deviate for a moment and discuss our government's need to increase the supply of money. We all have, quite often, talked about "monetary policy." Just try to get a standard definition of that one. I'll try my hand at it in a few paragraphs. First, let's debase the currency.

Our government soon found out it couldn't live within its means. One way to have more was to simply reduce certain precious metals in its coins and mix in other contents—produce more with less. The government would call in the gold, melt it down, reconfigure it and reissue more coins of lower value. The natural result was inflation. You have more money chasing after the same goods. This was the first go-round, and this process continued until the coin was no longer widely used.

Just wait until we get to the printing presses—working on three eight-hour shifts. Congress throughout our history had moments where they could not or would not balance the budget, and the inflationary results of their solutions are legion.

The need is to find equilibrium between what the government takes in and what it expends. One way is for the (National) Federal Reserve Bank to buy U.S. debt (bonds). But where does the cash come from? It doesn't come from anywhere. The U.S. Treasury account is credited. Simply put, debt is bought with nothing. The problem of balancing income and expenses has been "monetized."

The plot thickens with this newly created (not earned) money on account. The Treasury Department just writes checks on it. Don't make this part complicated. They write checks that look like any other government checks—much like yours and mine—except we can't do this.

Now, banks take in this money and lend it out. But as most of you know banks can lend (or keep in reserve) much more than they have on deposit. What is it now, a 20% hold ratio? The economy is flooded with money not backed up by any standard or reserve. It is backed up by the "full faith and pledge (trust)" of the U.S. government.

Currently, we have a Federal Reserve Bank dedicated first to holding down inflation and second to making sure this economy doesn't go into a recession. It has more or less been effective. It does this, however, with "monetary policy" on the use of credit and debit controls to maneuver the economy on its course. As long as we have faith, it all works.

Problems have occurred quite often. After the Vietnam War the government did not turn off spending and the Federal Reserve did not turn off the spigots. The huge quantity of money in the early to mid-70s created double-digit inflation and interest rates of 18, 19, and for a brief while, even the low 20% range. Have you ever tried to finance a home at 18% interest? Payments soared, real estate took a hit. Car prices skyrocketed. Do you remember Jimmy Carter?

Creating money this way is dishonest and immoral, but it is relatively easy, and controllable by politicians. During the 70s investors sought out safe harbors (or hiding places) against these ravaging and damaging effects. Gold and silver prices soared. Remember gold at $800 an ounce? That soon ended, with tight money bringing down inflation and the Reagan Tax Cut bringing billions more into the treasury.

There is another way to fund the need for more money. The deficit (the difference between what the government spends and what it takes in) under Reagan was financed by the private sector buying bonds. Soon billions of dollars of U.S. debt were owned overseas. Many old concerns of "dumping" the debt back on the U.S. Treasury have been resolved, but still it is unsettling how much debt we have.

The real solution would be for the government to live within its means and start accelerating the payments on its multi-trillion dollar debt. Lower taxes would help—they always have. Leaner government is not a wish but a must. We need less monetary policy and more common sense.

A few more chronological facts and historical asides will bear this out. In 1913, the Internal Revenue Act was passed. This let government intrude into the lives of private citizens beyond any fears our founding fathers had. The IRS started simply, but grew into a monstrosity. High, confiscatory taxes were transferred from the producers to the non-producers. Then Congress, the Fed, and others, with an unlimited ability to create paper money, raided trust funds for Social Security and amassed gargantuan federal debt and deficits. The process started in 1913. Only a gold-backed dollar blocked the way. As you'll soon see, our gold standard too would soon be a thing of the past.

First, after World War I, gold was discontinued as the means of settling international debt. The American dollar and the British pound became "proxy gold." In 1933, President Roosevelt passed a new regulation prohibiting Americans from holding gold. Citizens faced a ten-year jail term and a $10,000 fine for noncompliance—plus their gold was confiscated. Our benevolent government at its best. Soon thereafter the dollar was devalued by about 50%. It now took twice as many dollars to buy a house, twice as many pennies to buy bread. This restriction lasted 42 years. The government had all the gold, Americans got paper—and a request for more faith. Soon "In God We Trust" made it back on our paper currency.

The next setback for using gold as our monetary standard came with the Britton Woods Agreement at the close of the Second World War. With this agreement came the institution of the IMF (International Monetary Fund) and the World Bank. I can think of no two organizations that have hurt so many people, kept millions in poverty, and hurt the cause of global peace.

Their policies stink. Simply put, what undeveloped countries need, and definitely what industrial economies need, is cutting taxes and less government control—not more. The very things the IMF and the World Bank demand doom economies to failure. They are bad and should be eliminated.

Under Eisenhower, the restriction on Americans holding gold extended to Americans overseas. The relentless pursuit of stupidity continued.

Remember the $35 per ounce rate set by the government? In the 1950s there were more paper dollars overseas than gold being held to back it up. Some European countries started converting their dollars back to gold—the price for gold went above $35 per ounce. Free market economics were not dead.

In the mid '60s the LBJ "gang in charge" stopped minting silver coins. Why? The silver content was worth more than the face value of the coin. New coins with less silver were minted. What about the dollar?

In 1970, the dollar was still backed by a 25% gold storage. This 25% was eliminated. The dollar abroad was no longer redeemable in gold. The Nixon gang saw to that.

In the early years of the Nixon administration, several dark and devious things happened in the Democratic Congress.

With this latest debasing of the dollar, its value went plunging. Inflation worldwide was overheating. Stupidity now reigned supreme. Wages and price controls were imposed. What a low point for brain power. Under President Ford and "Whip Inflation Now," the dollar continued to plunge. Carter's remedy (what remedy?) was a joke—tight money talk, but the action was worse.

A temporary good side effect occurred. Under Jimmy Carter (or with his help), the Federal Reserve raised the discount rate to the point that businesses could borrow from the private sector cheaper than borrowing from the Fed, and money poured back into the treasury.

With Reagan and his reduction in tax rates, the government took in more money. This was a huge outflow of dollars to other countries, and the dollar stopped its slide. But remember the piper (our U.S. debt, held by foreigners) had to be paid? Now a convergence of seemingly good things created a recession.

Let me explain: The dollar strengthened against other currencies; cheaper foreign goods flooded in; oil prices went way down and, in short, inflation died. Then bam, the recession of 1982 with an increase in unemployment off the charts.

By the end of the year the Fed once again lowered the discount rate—made credit easier, and the economy and the stock market took off.

We have had such tinkering to varying degrees since time immemorial. Only of late have computers helped the tinkerers tinker more. The results? What do you think? We have run deficits every year since 1960, with the exception of 1969 (the height of the Vietnam War). Even now, the last year of this century and millennium, do we have a complete list of the IRA Trust Fund so the gang in the White House and other shortsighted people can boast of a budget surplus?

If our elected politicians are not able to control spending with or without a balanced budget amendment, we will continue to see a manipulation of the system. Monetary policy affects how the dollar behaves. The boom and bust cycles will continue.

Will we return to a gold standard? Not in our lifetime. Once in a while a "gold bug" speaks up and gets placed in the back editorial section of the *Wall Street Journal*, where they are hardly read. Sense would be made out of nonsense, but the gold standard system—from the Federal Reserve down to the member banks, from Capitol Hill to Main Street, it is not going to come back. There is about one gold statement of support for each 20 or so "monetarist" statements protecting the current status quo.

A VIEW OF THE CRASH OF 1987

The years from the crash of 1929 to 1987 were very eventful for gold. In spite of the fact that Americans were not able to hold gold for over 40 of those years, gold was still a player in the world marketplace.

The government repealed the 50% tax on profits from silver. They also suspended the issuance of silver coins (the 90% silver content ones). Political uncertainty was everywhere, seen in the Second World War, the long and drawn out cold war, the division of Germany, Russian and Chinese expansionist policy, and the Vietnam War.

Toward the end of the 1970s, gold prices soared. This rapid increase, as mentioned elsewhere, was on the heels of double-digit inflation. Soon, however, in 1982, the prices on gold, silver, and platinum were way back down. Ironically, a long bull market commenced at this time. Precious metal prices, except for silver, rebounded to a higher level.

Then, one fine day in October 1987, the 19th to be exact, buying stocks stopped. Many people to this day have tried to fix blame on something. Here are a few of the bad guys:

1. Foreigners quit buying our debt.

2. Program trading was responsible.

3. Overseas markets were overheated, then crashed. Many markets kept their doors closed.

4. Tight money talk, to curb inflation, had been turned into higher rates for months (even years) preceding the crash. (By the way, I agree with this one.)

Whatever the cause, or grouping of causes, the specialists on the floor were without buyers. Computer brokers were not answering the phone. The market fell 508 points in one day. Option trading halted, stock index futures stopped trading.

FEAR AND PANIC SPREAD

On Tuesday the 20th, with many exchanges closed, the Dow Jones Industrial Average fell another 100 points and looked like it was headed for complete disaster, but lo and behold, it came back. The market (DJIA index—one of the only markets still trading) rallied.

A few things happened. Several companies announced they would be buying back their stock. This was positive, but nothing like what was going on behind the scenes.

To get the full impact of this, you have to realize how much buying is done with debt. Bank loans to major brokerage houses, margin investing had run rampant because of the bull market mentality—but now the collateral was gone.

The Fed came to the rescue. The Federal Reserve stepped in with billions of dollars to shore up the banks. Once those key players knew there was a safety net, the hemorrhaging stopped. The market bounced back. Within a year or so it was higher than before.

The lesson we've learned has a sad side effect. We know Uncle Sam is there. The corrections needed from time to time are dishonest. The price we pay is in the uncertainty about the true value of the market. We have some peace of mind knowing they will step in with cash and protect the market.

What can we do? Well, several other chapters of this book deal with that. Let me add two quick but powerful ending thoughts.

1. I've said it before, I'll say it a hundred times. We (that means you and me) need to stay on the gold standard: accumulate for emergencies, have enough to last a typical crisis—three months to two years—collect easily marketable coins, stay the course, don't despair. Make our life "as good as gold."

2. I don't want to get mushy here, but there is a need to trust in God and keep our priorities right. Come what may, all will be with us when we do good for God. Nations will

come and go. Politicians will rise and fall. Bull and bear markets will be with us a long time. But through it all, we need to put God first, our families second, and the pursuit of wealth third. If the first two are correct, the last one will take care of itself.

Your gold and silver is cankered; and the rust of them shall be a witness against you, and shall eat your flesh as it were fire. Ye have heaped treasure together for the last days.

James 4:3

That the trial of your faith, being much more precious than of gold that perisheth, though it be tried with fire, might be found unto praise and honour and glory at the appearing of Jesus Christ.

Peter 1:7

I counsel thee to buy of me gold tried in the fire, that thou mayest be rich; and white raiment, that thou mayest be clothed, and that the shame of thy nakedness do not appear; and anoint thine eyes with eyesalve, that thou mayest see.

Revelation 3:18

 # VOCABULARY

I've put this vocabulary list up front as Chapter Four so you have a good understanding of the terms used in the gold industry. I have not included mining, panning, or gold and silver processing terms. This is interesting reading. Don't skip this.

Alloy
A metal with two or more elements. Gold or silver less than .999 percent purity is an alloy.

Avoirdupois
The weight system used in the United States; for example "lb." for pounds. This system is not used for gems and minerals.

Carat
A measurement unit used for gems. The root word is the same as for "Karat." The weight unit of one carat is 200 milligrams.

Bullion

Gold or silver considered in mass rather than in value. Usually in the form of bars or ingots.

Dore Bullion

An inferior alloy produced at the mine.

Fine

A measurement of the purity of a precious metal, in 1,000 parts.

Fine Ounce

A troy ounce, or 999/1,000 pure.

Grade

The quantity of gold or silver in a metric ton or ore.

Karat

A jewelry measurement for the fineness of gold. 24-karat is pure gold. This level of fineness would be too soft for typical jewelry.

Lode

From the word lead, a vein or deposit of ore or rocks containing the mineral being mined.

Metallurgy

The practice and study of extracting metals and the production of alloys. The study of their relationships.

Obverse

The front side or face of a coin.

Proof Coin

An extremely shiny coin produced for collectors; normally kept that way by being encased.

Pure Gold

.999 fineness or gold containing no other elements (not an alloy); also said of silver.

Restrike

A coin made with the original die-cut, but many years later.

Reverse

The backside of a coin.

Troy Ounce

31.103 grams.

Tellurides

Minerals where gold is located. Tellurium is similar to sulfur.

Ton

Short ton = 2,000 pounds

Metric Ton = 2,204.6 pounds

Long Ton = 2,240 pounds

5 INVESTING IN GOLD

I have been a big believer in gold since 1973, when I first started buying gold. I love gold investing. I believe that most people have missed out on an opportunity for peace of mind and security by not investing in gold.

Because there have been a number of problems and now with a "the sky is falling" type of problem in Y2K, I say, "Well, good!" Maybe now, with all these potential problems, people will take a second look at gold. "Hear! Hear!" Finally, someone will take my gold seminar seriously.

So now I would like to give you a good understanding of how to invest in gold, and then in a later chapter we will discuss further strategies and methods of investing.

WHY GOLD?

For thousands of years gold has been a store of value. I don't think that when most people contemplate an investment they consider gold as a candidate. You would usually think of an investment as being rental real estate, or stock and bonds. These are traditional investments.

Gold is an incredible metal. In and of itself, it is valuable. Why? Because gold can be used for so many things. For thousands of years, gold has been a marketable item. People have been able to trade gold for things they want and need like food, shelter, and services. Gold is literally one of the oldest mediums of exchange in the history of mankind. In the Bible, by the way, there are 25 references to the word gold. It has been around a long time.

Gold has many industrial uses. Most of you can think of a few uses for gold. You have seen it used in many ways. I'm sure you are aware of how popular gold is in jewelry. Why is that? There are other metals that are even more precious and rare than gold. Why gold?

One of the reasons that gold has been used in so many commercial and industrial applications is because of its malleability, which means its pliability. It is soft. It can be heated to a certain extent and still keep together. For example, I read recently that there has been one continuous long wire, 35 miles long, made of gold. Gold can be very thin; it can be produced in flat level sheets of 1/250,000th of an inch thickness.

As a matter of fact, here is something I find amazing as to how thin they can produce these sheets. I hope this amazes somebody else because it is mind-boggling to me. If you take a traditional Bible and measure its thickness, you will find that it is about an inch and a half or two inches thick, depending on the thickness of the paper, and how large the pages are. It is possible to take the whole Bible and put it on these very thin sheets of gold and literally write or have it engraved with microscopic type instruments. If you were to do this, the whole Bible would be reduced to about 1/16th of an inch thick, because these sheets are so thin. This is amazing!

NASA has even used gold on the outside of spacecrafts, because it won't interact with other metals that are bombarding the hull of the craft. It is an awesome, unique metal.

Gold is everywhere. Virtually every state in the United States has had mining operations or gold finds. Most countries in the world have access to gold deposits.

Let's discuss the cost of manufacturing gold. It is my belief that you should be investing in American Eagle gold bullion coins rather than other countries' coins. I will make a case for other countries too, but rather than gold nuggets or gold dust as we will discuss in another chapter, the place that you should put your money is in gold coins.

My point here, however, is that gold is found almost everywhere.

Traditionally, the most common place gold is found is in the crevices of rocks deep down in the earth. If you have ever seen a gold deposit, you will realize that it is usually found in rocks. There are little strings of gold (veins) in these rocks—little layers of gold embedded between other materials. It doesn't look the same as pyrite, which is artificial or "fool's gold." It doesn't resemble that at all.

As the rocks tumble down the streams in California, Alaska and other places, the gold deposits in these rocks are broken up and just tumble along, and go to the bottom of the stream. That is why you see people out panning for gold, even today. There is a whole industry of people trying to recover gold.

Recently there has been a worldwide glut of gold. Gold prices have come way down.

The "spot price" can be defined as the going price, set by the major exchanges. You will never pay the spot price for gold. At your local coin dealer you will pay spot (which fluctuates every day) plus about $20, as a premium, per ounce.

WHAT GOLD BUYS

In the 1920s, you could take out a handful of gold coins and buy a house for say $3,000.

Take the amount of gold that was necessary to buy a house in the 1920s or even in the 1950s, and now come forward 30 to 60 years and have in your hand the same handful of gold. If you took that same amount of gold that it took to build a house back then and go into the average neighborhood today, you could still buy the same house. But $3,000 would not even supply the down payment.

Is the 1920s too long ago for you? Then let's move to the 1950s or early 1960s. Houses were going for around $12,000 in newer subdivisions like you see in movies like *Back to the Future*. The amount of gold in 1963 that it took to buy an $8,000 to $12,000 house, today would still buy the house and go for $120,000 to $180,000. But $12,000, again, would barely make the down payment.

Here's the point. It is not that gold has gone up in value, it is that the dollar has gone so far down in value. That is the point of investing in gold. Let me say that again. *It is not that gold has gone so far up in value, it is that the dollar has gone so far down in value.* It takes so many more dollars to buy what we used to buy for fewer dollars.

I'll give you proof of this change in value. How many of you remember going to movies when you were a kid for 25¢? (I've even had older students in seminars who went for a nickel or a dime, but that was before my time.) One quarter to get into a movie. A quarter! Today a movie costs $7 and $8. And, by the way, there were a lot better movies back then for a quarter than we get today for $8. You got a lot more value for your quarter. But it is this concept—that it takes so many more dollars to buy the same things—that should pique our interest in owning gold.

This is one reason for investing in gold. Gold will keep pace with inflation, and even set the pace of inflation. Let me say that again—gold and real estate have been the pacesetters for inflation. Why not invest in gold today?

Back in early 1920, gold was trading for around $16 an ounce. You could take a gold coin into a men's clothing store and buy a nice men's suit. You could also take $16 cash in and buy the same men's suit. Today, if you were to have that same gold coin, which is trading for $300, $320, or $340 an ounce, and go into a men's clothing store, you could still buy a nice men's suit. But what would $16 buy? Socks, maybe. Again, it's not that gold has gone up in value, it is that the dollar has gone down in value.

When you talk about dollars, is not the dollar a measurement of, or a representation of some store of value that is being held in reserve to protect it, like gold used to be? How many people remember seeing Silver Certificates? Today paper currency says, "Federal Reserve Note." For many years, in the very early part of our country when they used Silver Certificates, "In God We Trust" was on everything. Then paper money was actually tied to a metal. When we did away with the gold standard, when there was no more gold or silver standard to base the paper currency upon, they put the words "In God We Trust" back on the paper currency. We can't trust in Fort Knox. We can't trust in any store of value representing our backing up our pieces of paper. The only trust we have is in God.

PLATINUM

Now a lot a people say, why gold? Why not platinum? Platinum is between $30 to $50 per ounce more expensive than gold, and I have even heard recently that it has gone as high as $80 an ounce more. It's wonderful if you want to own platinum. To a certain extent platinum looks like silver. I don't own a lot of platinum because I want to own gold. There are millions of gold collectors around the world, but not very many platinum collectors. If you are going to buy and sell something on a rapid basis, you want to have access to as wide a market as possible.

GOLD IN YOUR IRA

You can own gold in your pension plan and in your IRA, if it is a self-directed IRA. Now, the only problem is getting up a little agreement between you, as a person owning a self-directed IRA, and you as a person holding the gold. Where are you going to store it? In a safety deposit box somewhere? Fine, do that. I have chosen in my own life not to own gold in my IRA. However, about every fourth or fifth time I'm at the coin dealer, somebody walks in with a check for $32,000 from their IRA to the coin dealer to buy all kinds of gold and silver. People may own gold in their IRAs, but the only gold and silver you can own in your IRA is government-minted coins. Why? Because it has been assayed. There is a certain level of quality that exists in coins, and therefore it can be held in your IRA and it's not just somebody's guess what it is worth.

HEDGE AGAINST INFLATION

Buying gold is not only a hedge against inflation, but it can also be rewarding and educational. Do we need gold as a hedge against inflation? Yes, but gold does not earn interest. It does not collect rent. It is not a traditional form of investment with dividends and earnings. Gold is a piece of metal that you put in a drawer or a safety deposit box or some other safe place. That's all there is to keeping it. It is hassle free.

1 oz. American Eagle

1 oz. American Eagle
1889

1 oz. American Eagle
1893

1 oz. American Eagle
1897

1 oz. American Eagle   1/2 oz. U.S. Gold

1/4 oz. U.S. Gold   1/10 oz. U.S. Gold

1 oz. Indian Head   1 oz. Liberty

Old Eagle   Silver Trade Unit

1 oz. Panda

China Panda

Australian Platinum
Nugget

Australian Nugget
(Kangaroo)

Canadian Maple Leaf   Russian Chervonets

Australian Nugget   Hungarian Korona

Silver Certificate

Collector's set of proof coins

Collector's set of proof coins

*Spare minutes are the gold-dust of time; the portions of
life most fruitful in good or evil; the gaps through which
temptations enter.*

—Anonymous

 # BUYING GOLD
COINS

Now that we've gone over the importance and history of
gold and have a little background on gold investment, let's learn
how to build up our own gold portfolio. As we've discussed in
the previous chapters, the value of gold paces and even sets the
rate of inflation. Since it's almost guaranteed that inflation will
continue, it's a good idea to have 5% to 10% of your assets in gold
to hedge against the falling value of the dollar. With this in mind,
collecting gold in the form of coins proves to be the best value for
your money.

NUMISMATICS

"Numismatics" is the term we use for the study and collection of coins. There is a whole group of people who are interested
in collecting gold coins based on their history, rarity, quality and
condition. Professionals rate these coins according to "numismatic
value."

A traditional gold dealer would try to get you to buy coins for
this objective. He may direct your attention, for example, to an

old, turn-of-the-century coin valued for the French artwork. If the price of gold were $300 an ounce, instead of $310 or $320, you would have to pay upwards of $400 (or even more) because of its numismatic value.

You will learn real fast that Wade Cook is different. I collect gold for the sole purpose of owning the metal. I really don't care about the extra numismatic value. Now, I do own a few coins for their origin and artistry, but I mainly own these rare coins to display at my seminars and demonstrate how the artwork has developed over the years. Other than that, I don't want to have a whole lot of coins that have an ambiguous, arbitrary value of an extra $50, $100 or $150 premium per coin based on somebody else's opinion of it. When I go into a coin dealership, I go in with the intention of buying for the gold content, period.

I don't think average investors should concern themselves with anything beyond the intrinsic gold value in coins. Of course, some of you may be interested and want to become an expert at numismatic investing. Like any other type of investment, whether it is in the stock market or in real estate, there's a wealth of information available for you to study and master. You can visit any coin dealer or go to any bookstore and pick up useful information. I'm sure the dealers would love to have more investors trying to make money on gold coins. Personally, I just don't see a lot of money to be made there, and I don't believe that it's a viable way or reason for owning gold, especially for the novice.

AMERICAN GOLD COINS

The oldest U.S. gold coins that I've been able to get a hold of are from the 1880s. These coins are just beautiful. The fine artwork was done in France and then minted onto the American coins. They are known as "American Eagles" because of the huge eagle printed on the back. On the front side of the coin today is a lady in a dress, or "Walking Liberty." From about 1880 to about 1904 or 1907, Lady Liberty was simply depicted as a woman's head.

On newer coins the eagle image is slightly different, with one eagle flying back to the nest, where a second eagle waits with the babies. If you look at coins minted from the late 1880s to the 1920s, you'll see slight changes in design as the years go by.

This brings us to the Roaring Twenties. As we covered before, our government virtually made it illegal for Americans to own gold or gold coins. The gold collected from U.S. citizens was melted down, made into bullion bars and stored at Fort Knox. During that period, the U.S. Mint ceased to operate and did not resume production until 1986. What happened in 1986 that changed everything? Before 1986, you could buy gold coins from a few countries throughout the world that were still minting and making gold coins available. The United States observed how much money was being raised in those foreign countries from the sale of their coins. Since our country had hundreds of billions of dollars in debt at the time, the government saw an opportunity to pay off some of the debt by going back to minting. They planned to mint new coins from the gold stored at Fort Knox and use part of the profits from sales to reduce the massive federal debt.

American coins are referred to as gold "bullion" because they are not entirely pure. You often see people on TV on those old cowboy shows finding gold and biting it with their teeth. Don't do that—it hurts! Believe me, I've tried. Gold is actually very hard in a nugget or solid form. However, pure gold, or 24 karat gold, is relatively soft and will scratch very easily. Due to this fact, the United States Mint decided to harden up the gold a bit by mixing in two harder metals. This reduced the quality of the gold down to 22 karats. However, the gold is still around 99+% pure. The American Eagle coin is 22 karat gold and weighs 1.1 ounces, or one troy ounce.

MINTING COINS: AGAIN

We have with us still thousands of coins from the early years of our Republic. Those have numismatic value of varying amounts.

In 1792, Congress authorized the minting of silver coins. In 1795, gold was added. These were done at the Philadelphia mint. The San Francisco mint opened in 1854. The Carson City Mint opened in the 1870s and produced both gold and silver coins.

Now that Americans can own gold again, the government started minting gold coins in 1986.

The coins are 1 oz., $^1/_2$ oz., $^1/_4$ oz., and $^1/_{10}$ oz. The coins trade at a slight premium to their gold content value, and much higher than the dollar denomination listed on the obverse side.

Listed Dollar Value	Content (Gold)	Weight
$50	1 oz.	1.0909 troy ounce
$25	$^1/_2$ oz.	0.5455 troy ounce
$10	$^1/_4$ oz.	0.2727 troy ounce
$ 5	$^1/_{10}$ oz.	0.1091 troy ounce

OTHER COUNTRIES

Many other countries mint gold coins. South Africa has the Krugerrand. Canada has the Maple Leaf. China has the Panda, England has the Britannia, and Australia has the Nugget (looks like a nugget in the shape of Australia).

Coins, especially those produced by governments, provide the collector several benefits. Besides the beauty, they are marketable as a medium of exchange and can be readily converted to cash. Conversely, these coins can be held in retirement accounts, whereas gold dust or nuggets may not.

The different editions of these coins, made in different quantities, may also increase a coin's investment value. These coins are legal tender.

CHANGING PRICES

Prices change everyday, giving everyone a certain stability in trading. Dips also provide buying opportunities. Just as gold price fluctuations have daily changes, there are also several things that change the value of gold over a longer period of time.

Simply put, just as the stock market has bear and bull periods, so the gold market has similarly named periods. What are they and what has caused them (in the past), and what can we look for?

The past is present is future. Bear markets in gold are caused by several factors. These do not need to be in tandem.

1. When the economy is sailing along, and the stock market is soaring, a complacent feeling takes over and people think they don't need gold.

2. Governments, to raise cash, sold billions of dollars of gold and flooded the world wide market. Usually, too much supply causes brief downturns.

3. Huge new supplies (finds) are added to the market place—with cheaper and better mining and processing.

In short, all above ground supplies are suspect. If abnormal amounts are sold, the price goes down. All government hoards are potentially bearish as a government can sell at any time. When they do sell, the price goes down worldwide until the overage is absorbed.

BULLISH FACTORS

1. The sheer fact that governments are once again minting coins means that their stock piles are becoming smaller—mostly quite slowly.

2.   Collectors and investors are on the rise. For example, the first gold coin mintage (1986) was sold out. This pulls gold off the market.

3.   With economic unrest and world wide uncertainties, a fair number of people and governments will turn to gold.

4.   The new Y2K problem and gold ownership have somehow gotten connected. This will have a profound but temporary affect. I hope to be one who continues to promote gold to this new group of people, who may want to continue to own and collect it into the new millennium.

5.   Gold is beautiful. As economies rise and people have more spendable income, jewelry and other uses will grow.

6.   Gold is a versatile metal. People and governments will always be creative with their uses of this precious resource.

7.   The current monetary system is still scary and in high places everywhere there are "gold-bugs." As talk of a return to a gold standard surfaces from time to time, gold consumption, collection and hoarding will rise.

BULLISH OR BEARISH

Perceptions change. Even though there are fluctuations in gold prices, all in all the price will be controlled by supply and demand. These fluctuations give many buying opportunities. It's easy to chart gold. It's easy to buy on dips.

 # BUY RIGHT

There are four denominations of coins minted in the United States gold bullion set: one ounce, one-half ounce, one-quarter ounce and one-tenth ounce. The smaller coin denominations, including the one-tenth ounce and even the quarter ounce, are not a big medium of exchange. They are almost always reserved for jewelry. You see these coins in pendants, bracelets, et cetera. For example, I have a ring with a Mexican gold peso of a little less than a quarter ounce. I think everyone should stick only with buying one-ounce coins, even if it requires saving up a little bit more. This is where you get the best value.

A lot of people think that if they don't have enough money to buy a one-ounce coin, they might as well go ahead and buy a quarter ounce or a one-tenth ounce coin. Let's look at why this isn't such a hot idea. If a one-ounce coin is going for $320, in theory the half-ounce coin should go for $160, that is, half the one-ounce price. The half ounces actually go for $175. You see, you're paying a premium for the smaller denominations. In the same vein, you would think the quarter ounces would go for $80 ($320 divided by 4), but they really go for $90. Instead of going for $32 ($320 divided by 10), the one-tenth ounce coins are $40. Now, my numbers may be a few dollars off, but do you see the problem here? You are never going to get back your price in the actual gold content because you are paying such a high premium for those smaller denominations. What this all boils down to is that you should save up your money until you can afford the one-ounce pieces. Stay away from the fractions.

Probably 95% of all of my gold coins are American Eagle gold bullion coins. I prefer to buy American Eagles because they are government-minted coins. Unlike gold nuggets or gold dust, these gold coins do not have to be assayed when you try to sell them. The minimum cost for an assay exam is about $35 to $40, but it usually costs around $60 to $70. If you are going to get three or four ounces of gold assayed just so you can sell it to someone, the cost will eat right into most of your profits. Another advantage to buying American Eagle coins is that you can own them in an IRA. As I stated earlier, most Americans don't realize that. You can own gold in a self-directed IRA or pension plan as long as it is government-minted. Coins in this category have already been assayed and are guaranteed to hold up to a certain level of quality.

FOREIGN COINS

Sometimes it's just plain fun to own coins from around the world. I pick them up from time to time because they are interesting to me. For example, I have a whole set of four coins from the Cook Islands because my last name is Cook. I am going to make a case for staying away from foreign coins, however. Before we go into that, let me describe some of the more common foreign coins so that you can recognize them.

The first coin we'll talk about is the Austrian $^1/_2$ ounce. The gold is very, very thin, but the artwork is exquisite.

The Russian Chervonets bears the image of a man standing with a bag throwing seeds out over a field. I don't know exactly how much gold is in this coin, but I would venture to say that the gold content is probably between 18 and 20 karats. It is almost a purple color, it's diluted so much.

Chinese coins are called Pandas. Virtually every one of these has a picture of a great temple on one side, and on the other side are pandas in various poses. You can see the beautiful brushed artwork on the Panda.

Canadian Maple Leafs have a big maple leaf on the back and a picture of Queen Elizabeth on the front. It is 24 karats and weighs exactly one ounce. The Maple Leaf is thicker but with a circumference slightly smaller than the American Eagle. The Maple Leafs are pure gold. Visit a coin shop and look at the difference in color between a Mapleleaf and an American Eagle. The Maple Leaf is much more yellow.

Gold coins minted in Australia are called Nuggets. Some coins have a picture of what looks like a rock or nugget on the back, but that is actually the shape of Australia. Even if you get an Australian gold coin that has a picture of a wallaby or kangaroo on it, it is still called an Australian Nugget.

I also have a beautiful Australian platinum coin with a mother koala with her baby on her back climbing a tree.

As I mentioned, I own a number of foreign coins as curiosities, but the majority of my coins are American Eagles. Remember that I invest in gold for gold content value only. It doesn't matter whether the American Eagles were minted in 1993 or 1992 or 1986; they are all going for the same dollar. Foreign coins, on the other hand, go for varying, higher premiums because of their numismatic value.

For example, I once saw a beautiful half-ounce Australian coin and paid an extra $6 premium for it. I was willing to pay the $6 for the beautiful artwork. However, if there was a time of crisis or emergency and I wanted to sell it for the cash, I would not be able to collect back that $6 in premium. The premium has no basis in reality except for somebody's opinion of it. That's why you should be very careful when you buy gold.

WHERE AND HOW

Where do you find them? How much should you pay for them? Where do you store them once you get them? First let's talk about how to buy them. It is not complicated. This whole system of buying gold coins is quite simple. All you have to do is get out your Yellow Pages and look up "gold" or "gold dealers" or "coin dealers." Nowadays, many coin dealers have all their coins in one case. They are usually found in the backs of T-shirt shops or baseball card shops. The main business is in buying and selling baseball cards, football cards and basketball cards, while the gold business is on the side.

If you have a chance, you should also visit a coin show when they come to town. Typically, 80 to 120 different coin dealers get together and rent a hall for a couple of days. Buy books from these dealers, study them, and get to know them. Coin shows are sometimes where I get my best deals. Why? Here you have around 120 coin dealers in one place, and half the dealers there may sell nothing but American Eagle gold coins. They are all in competition with each other to pick you up as a customer. At the last coin show I went to, the price for gold was at about $360 to $380 an ounce. I was able to negotiate the prices down so that I only paid $2 to $4 over spot price instead of $20 like I normally pay.

I mentioned something called the "spot price." This is the set price for gold on any given day, and it can change throughout the day. It usually doesn't change that much, but it definitely can change 50¢ to a dollar throughout a day. Where does this spot price come from? Gold prices are set in Hong Kong at the beginning of every day. The prices are transmitted from Hong Kong to the London Exchange and then from London to the New York Exchange, called COMEX.

I think there are about 32 major dealers licensed by the U.S. Mint to handle the trading of gold coins in America. All the other coin dealers you see are tied to these 32 dealers personally or electronically in some way. So, even in the gold coin industry there is a middleman. When you talk about moving hundreds or even thousands of particular coins each day, even a dollar on a coin, it can add up to a substantial amount of money over a period of time.

Let's go back to your local coin dealer's office. Depending upon what kind of customer you are (big or small), the coin dealer is going to charge you spot price plus somewhere around $20 to buy gold. When you ask him about the price of gold, he will jump on his computer or call an 800 number. The people on the other end of the 800 number will tell him gold's spot price at that time. If gold is at $298, he's going to tell you a price of $318 when he gets off the phone. In other words, he is going to charge you a premium. Now, if you are a brand new customer or you come in only once or twice a year, most coin dealers are going to charge you between $22 and $25 on top of spot. This is just common business sense. If you are a better customer, the dealers will lower the price. My coin dealer normally charges me between $15 and $18 because I buy so many coins from him. If, however, I go in and want to buy 10 or 15 coins at a time, he'll give me spot plus $10 or $12.

Awhile ago I wanted to order several hundred ounces of gold. We're talking $75,000 or $80,000 worth of gold in one purchase. I told the dealer that I would pay spot plus $4 and buy 250 ounces. So just for making one phone call, getting the gold delivered and handing it over to me, the dealer made $1,000 for 5 or 6 minutes of work. I was able to demand my price because of the quantity of the purchase. Most of us, though, are not going to get anywhere near that kind of price. As a rule of thumb, you are going to pay spot plus $20.

Like I said before, buying gold is easy. You go into the coin dealer with a little money, like $300 to $400. You tell him that you want to buy gold. He will give you the price, say $318 or $320, and then you just pay the money and get a receipt for it. That's all it is. It's that simple. And you walk out the door with your coin.

THINGS TO WATCH OUT FOR

I am not familiar with all the laws in every state, but I know that there are some troubling practices in some states, particularly California. I know about California because I go there all the time. The first thing I want to warn you about is taxes. Right now in the State of California, you must pay an 8.1% or 8.2% sales tax if you buy less than $1,000 worth of coins from a dealer. However, if you buy over $1,000 worth of coins at one time, you do not have to pay the sales tax. Let's get specific. If you go into a coin shop and buy a one-ounce American Eagle for $320, you would end up paying somewhere around $25 more for the purchase (8% times $320 = $25.60) just on tax. What this means is that when you go to sell the coin, you have to have a huge swing in the gold price minus how much you get over spot to make any sort of profit. Once I went to a coin dealer in California and purchased $992 worth of coins. The dealer looked at me and said, "You need to buy $8 more, and then you don't have to pay the sales tax." Just going over the $1,000 limit would save me around $80 in tax!

The second thing I want to let you know about is registration. Some states, including California, want you to fill out a form to register your gold coins every time you buy. This is like registering your gun. Can you think of anything more stupid? You do not want to tell anybody that you have gold or where you keep it, let alone the government. You do not want to register your gold. The first time I came across this situation, the dealer handed me this piece of paper to fill out. I started writing in my name, but then I stopped and said to the guy, "Listen, I don't want to lie, but I'm not going to give you my name and address." I reasoned with him, "You're not going to check up on it. I'm not going to give it to you. So do I have to fill out this piece of paper?"

The dealer responded, "You absolutely do not have to fill out this piece of paper, but I, as a coin dealer, by state law, am required to give it to you."

"So what you're saying is that I as a citizen do not have to fill it out, but you as a dealer have to give it to me and request that I fill it out, but there is no law that says I have to comply?"

He answered, "That's correct."

So there you have it. The dealers will ask you to fill out the form and register, but you are under no obligation to grant the request. I, for one, am not going to tell any government agency where I have my money, especially gold coins that are highly transportable.

I've gone over the laws in California as they stand now, but laws change all the time. Other states have their own laws about the taxes, registration, and gold dealing, so educate yourself in the current laws of your state.

WHERE TO PUT IT

Now, the only issue remaining is where to store your gold. You need to find a good, safe place to put it. I'm really not big on the safety deposit boxes that you find at your local bank, and there is one main reason for that. There is a registry of each of these safety deposit boxes. If you owed money to the IRS or to the court, for example, they can just look for your name on the registry, go right to that bank and open up your box. There is virtually no safety through the U.S. banking system that way. This is not the place to keep the things you want kept in privacy.

You might want to consider storing your gold in a security depository, found in virtually every major city in this country.

These depositories are usually buried away so that about half the building is in the side of a hill or in some kind of rock formation. You can go into those places and pay anywhere from $50 a year to hundreds of dollars per year for a small, little safety deposit type box. The key thing to remember is that these depositories are not part of a federal registry system. I have my gold in these types of places in different cities. As I travel around the country, I like to go visit my money once in a while. I don't have all my gold in one place and I don't think anybody else should either. It's simply a matter of security. If you want to find one of these depositories, look under "Security" or "Safety" in the Yellow Pages. You can get a tour of the place. I'm not going to give you the name of the one I use, because then everyone around the country will come here and use that one and the rates will go up. But they are everywhere. Find one and keep your gold there.

One last thing—you may have seen advertisements for firms who are in the business of selling and storing gold. When you buy coins from them, they will store the actual coins in a vault somewhere and send you a certificate of gold deposit. In other words, you do not receive and keep the gold yourself. If you decide to invest in gold certificates, be very careful. I don't encourage you to do it, but if you do, make sure the firm is licensed and bonded. Many years ago, one of these big firms had $20 million worth of gold on file for their clients. All of a sudden a few people wanted their gold, and they discovered that the firm held only about $2 million worth of gold. The owners of this company had ripped off $18 million. They claimed to have been simply borrowing against the reserve and had every intent to pay it back at some time, but other parts of the business didn't go too well and they lost the $18 million. Everyone thought that they were licensed and bonded, but they were not. All the investors were left with was a piece of paper saying, "You have gold at this place." Always make sure where your gold is and be careful who has control of your money.

We have comforts that kings might consider luxuries, yet it is real punishment for us to stay at home; we have wealth and occupation, but little of that piece of mind surpassing wealth which the sage finds in meditation.
—Dr. Joseph Collins

 # YOUR PORTFOLIO

I have a really great system for buying gold. You might say to yourself, "Boy, I'd sure like to have $5,000 or $10,000 worth of gold," but many of you do not have the amount of cash necessary to go and buy that much. If you do, go for it! You probably would get a better deal, maybe spot plus $10. However, most Americans have a tough enough time paying the bills each month, and coming up with an extra $10,000 or so for gold can seem like an insurmountable task.

Let me tell you how I got started. I realized a long time ago that nothing is permanent. I was doing very well with my real estate investments and making a lot of money, but I knew that the circumstances supporting my real estate success might not last. It has lasted, by the way, but it still might not last forever. My solution was to diversify. That's what you should do. In other words, don't put all your money into one thing, like the stock market. If you do have a lot of money in the stock market, make sure you don't have it all in only one or two companies. You can put your money into real estate, either directly or indirectly. If you don't want to own real estate directly and collect the rents as a landlord, you can buy into a partnership or invest in REITS (Real Estate Investment Trust Units) or own stock in trusts and corporations that own real estate. You can also invest in coins, stamps, or anything else you'd like. I started looking into gold.

I was only 27 years old at the time, but I realized something about money. Now, all of you have received chunks of money before. Let's say you're a real estate agent and you get a commission check for $4,000. What happens to the money? It goes! Have you heard the latest about people who win millions of dollars in the lottery? Within two years, all the lottery money is gone and the winner is either deep in the hole or filing for bankruptcy. These lottery winners dramatically increase their standards of living and spend most of the money on depreciating assets. They end up with nothing. These people have not learned the correct principles of wealth. I suggest that you learn the principles of wealth. My stock market seminars are a good place to start, but there are other good seminars and plenty of books that you can study. Learn everything you can, not only making money, but also keeping it— with more emphasis on keeping it. See my book, *Brilliant Deductions,* for great ways to keep and preserve your assets.

This is the game I play. When I got out of the Air Force, I went home to Tacoma, Washington, and started buying and selling houses. Every time I finished up a deal, I would go down to the coin dealer in Tacoma with the money I made and buy a gold coin. The price of gold would go up and down each time I visited the coin dealer, but it didn't matter. One week it was at $240, the next week at $230, the next week at $250. No matter what the price, after every real estate closing I would get some cash out of the bank and go buy a coin. I never missed one. A year later after, about 46 closings, I had about 52 coins (since I occasionally bought more than one at a time). Imagine how much money I would have had to buy those 52 coins all at once. At an average of $200 apiece, that's $10,000 cash. I would have never been able to do it, and I would have never done it. As it turned out, using my system I never even missed the money.

I'm going to suggest that you buy gold in the same way. Go out and buy a coin with your paycheck, once a month. Even if you don't have enough in any given paycheck to buy a full ounce, save up and buy with every other paycheck. You can also reward yourself on a special deal with gold. For example, I buy myself one gold coin for every seminar I teach and ten gold coins for every book I write. Reward yourself for something you've done and buy a gold coin. Then just stash it away, under your bed, in a box. The point is that if you keep the money, $200 or $300 for each month of the year, rather than buying gold, it's going to disappear. If you have a couple of thousand dollars sitting in the bank, you can bet that it's going to be spent. Kids need braces, the car is in the shop, and a new pool is being built out back. There are a million reasons for the money to be spent, and then it's gone. Discipline yourself a little bit better so that every time you have extra money, you buy a gold coin. I've been playing this game since 1977 when I first started in real estate.

Don't keep all the fun to yourself. Gold coins make great gifts. If you are going to give a young couple a wedding gift of several hundred dollars, why not give them a one-ounce gold coin? Get them started collecting. I give gifts of gold coins all the time to friends and family members who have never owned one. Usually this will spark their interest in collecting. I've been teaching and preaching about investing in gold for 13 or 14 years, and sometimes the only way to get people interested is to get the gold into their hands. Spread the gold bug!

CASHING IN

Now, there will come a day when you absolutely need cash. Let's say you need to buy some groceries for the month and decide to sell one of your gold coins to come up with the money. Gold is easily convertible to cash. All you have to do is go to your coin dealer and cash in.

Assume you bought a coin for $318. The question here is what price would a dealer give you for the same ounce of gold? The answer is usually spot plus $3 to $5. Sometimes you can get spot plus $10; depending on how big of a supply is in the dealer's back room. In general, if gold is going for $298 an ounce on the spot, the dealer is going to give you $302 or $303 for it. Think back to how much you originally paid for it. Do you see the difference there? Can you see how coin dealers make their money? They profit from the difference in buying wholesale and selling retail. It is not a lot of money, really. Most of these coin dealers sell between one and five coins a day. How many coins would they have to sell a day to pay the rent, to pay themselves a salary, and maybe hire one or two employees? This is why they turn to baseball cards, which trade at a greater volume. They support themselves on baseball cards, while the few gold purchases are just extra gravy to them.

You could call up four coin dealers and ask, "I have five American Eagle gold coins to sell. What are you paying for them?" They will basically respond with something like, "Well, if they are in good condition, spot plus $4." Another dealer might say "Spot plus $5," and yet another person might tell you, "Spot plus $3." If the dealer giving the price of spot plus $5 is located 20 miles away, you might as well forget the extra dollar per coin and go to the guy offering $4. It's not worth it. Don't forget to look at circumstances other than price when making these deals.

Dealers base their prices on the spot, which can mean different returns at different times. Say a dealer buys a coin at $303, and the coin remains unsold for several weeks. If the price of gold goes up $10 or $15 in those weeks, the person who finally does buy it has to pay that much more money based on the new, elevated spot. If the spot stood at $320, the price would be $338 to $340. Thus, the dealer made extra money because the price of gold went up. Conversely, what if the dealer buys the coin at $340 and the spot goes down to $320? He is going to sell at a loss. However, I have never met a coin dealer who will not buy or sell at any given price, even if they lose money. The nature of the game is cash flow, and dealers just keep turning their money over all the time. Even if they sell to you at a little bit under the price they paid, they can buy from the next guy who walks in and sell two weeks later at a higher price. I've never had anybody refuse to buy or sell at the normal price on any given day, although a dealer is not obligated to buy our coins.

A NEW FUN STRATEGY—SILVER

There have been times in my life when I've had to sell a few of my gold coins just to pay the bills. I'll go and sell them, but I follow another one of my rules: don't leave the coin dealership lighter than when you went in. Whenever I sell an American Eagle gold bullion coin, I also buy a few silver Eagles for $6 or $7 each. Thus, I walk out heavier than when I walked in. I do the same thing when I have a little extra money after purchasing gold. If I have $400 cash and buy $380 worth of gold, I'll spend the extra $20 on silver. I have so many silver coins now that I could probably fill a good car trunk full, and the car wouldn't be able to move because it would be so heavy.

Let's talk about silver for a moment. I have a lot of silver American Eagle coins, but most of the silver I have is in 10 ounce bricks and one pound bricks. I usually buy silver coins minted in places like California and Wyoming where the coins are minted 99.9% pure. If silver is going for $4.60 an ounce; you can buy these coins for 40¢ or 50¢ over spot. On the other hand, you are going to pay $3 or $4 over spot for a U.S. minted American Eagle. That $3 or $4 discrepancy in premium is just not worth it to me, so that's why I don't actively seek out silver American Eagles. I would rather invest in silver coins from other mints, since I am mainly after the content value and nothing more.

GET GOING!

Gold investing is a lot of fun, but the true reward is in the protection you get against the falling value of the dollar. My advice right now is to get on a program and start accumulating your reserve. All you have to do is buy one ounce and you are on your way. Again, gold could and should represent about five percent of your net worth. If you're worth $100,000 dollars, you should have at least $5,000 in gold. If you are worth $1 million dollars, you should have $50,000 in gold. A lot of people feel more comfortable with 10% of their money in gold. That's fine. Go for it.

*It cannot be denied that outward accidents conduce much
to fortune; favor, opportunity, death of others, occasion
fitting virtue: but chiefly, the mold of a man's fortune is
in his own hands.*

—Francis Bacon

 PREPARING FOR A CRISIS

Earlier in this book, we talked about different aspects of gold, such as owning gold, how to buy it, and little games on how to get yourself into a method or a system of buying gold.

But, why gold at this time and in this place? Consider the following:

What would happen if there were a major trucking strike like we had many years ago? What would happen if all the railroads went on strike? How long do you think it would take before the store shelves emptied out? Not very long!

Right now in America, the average store has enough nonperishable food and supplies to last five weeks. That doesn't include the backup warehouses, but isn't that scary?

Even greater than the chance of having a trucking strike or a railroad strike, even greater than having some nationwide catastrophe like the Y2K crisis, there is the likelihood that you are going to have some kind of a personal or localized tragedy. A family member may have a car accident. The breadwinner of your family could be laid up for nine months. You could get a sickness that you never thought was possible. What are you doing to prepare for it? Catastrophes and tragedies are going to happen.

Tragedies. They happen all the time. You know they happen. So you know there's a likelihood that it's going to happen to you. Instead of worrying about the country in general, why don't you worry about just you and your family?

Y2K, once again, is just one small thing on the horizon that could have a dramatic affect on a few people if your company is not really ready for it. Personally, I think it will have a minimal effect because Yankee ingenuity is going to take over through 1999 and the first part of the year 2000. You will see literally tens of thousands of people trained to rise to the occasion in just a short period of time. You will see forces muster that you never thought possible.

This is America. Have we not met every challenge that we've been faced with? This country continually meets challenges that are a lot more serious and in depth in nature than this Y2K problem. We will rise to this occasion as well.

Now I am really glad that gold has once again come to the forefront. In addition to gold, there are specific things that I think every one of us can do to make sure we are ready for any kind of tragedy or crisis.

If there was a catastrophe, either nationally or in your own life, there are five things that I know you should be concerned about. Taking care of these five things can help you weather a catastrophe, whether on a personal level like the loss of your job, a local level like Hurricane Hugo, a national level like a war and economic downturn, or a global level like Y2K.

1. FOOD/PERSONAL SUPPLIES

The number one thing that I am afraid of is running out of food. If I'm going to have any type of storage at all, it will not be a great big supply of gold. It will be food. I've seen people chomp down on gold to test it, but it is not edible. So even though I think that gold is important, it is much more important to me to have food to eat. Good, workable, usable food. Canned food, dried food, or other food that will stay in existence for a long time.

Recently, I came into contact with a gentleman through a distribution company that our publicly traded company purchased. I think that he is just an absolutely remarkable person. His name is James Stevens. He is the author of a book called *Making The Best Of Basics* (Gold Leaf Press, $19.95, 1-888-467-4446). I think everybody in the country should have this book.

It is not designed to be a reading book; it is designed to be a reference book. If you need to learn about fuels, if you need to learn about food, if you need to learn about money, this guy has it down. By the way, he also has a new book called, *Don't Get Caught With Your Pantry Down*. It's important that you take the time to educate yourself with this kind of information.

WIPE-O-PHOBIA

Without sounding too gross, I'll tell you what I'm really afraid of running out of.

If this economy was in a downturn, there was a trucking strike, and there was a lack of stuff in the store, I would be deathly afraid of running out of toilet paper. When I think about those old guys using pinecones and stuff like that back in the time of Daniel Boone, and I don't even want to imagine what they used in the deserts of Egypt before toilet paper came around. I know other people might be laughing, but for me it is toilet paper.

Now, I don't know what you buy, or where you spend all of your money, but I'll tell you what: instead of buying that extra present for $36, I'd rather spend $29, and up to $54 nowadays, to buy a case of toilet paper.

I'm serious. I could be considered an expert on toilet paper, because I am not going to run out of toilet paper if any kind of crisis ever comes. I've got enough toilet paper now to last for a year or two.

Plus, I figure they're going to say, "I'm a little bit hungry, but you know that Cook guy's got toilet paper!" It's called diversification at a whole new level.

But seriously, you need to think not just about food, but what other things you need to survive. For you and your family it may be extra diapers, or prescriptions, or _____ (you fill in the blank). Think about what else is personally important for you to stockpile.

WHAT ABOUT BOOKS?

If you were shut up for three days, or three months, or three years, one of the biggest requests on your list should be good reading material in your home for you and your kids. Your VCR may not work. I see people who have a year's supply of videos to watch, and software programs and computer programs, but if there's no electricity for awhile, guess what? We are back to good old-fashioned books.

I encourage you to develop a really good reading and reference library. In addition to *Making the Best of Basics* and *Don't Get Caught With your Pantry Down*, which I mentioned earlier, there are literally hundreds of good books out there about survival in adverse conditions: cookbooks, first aid books, plant identification, et cetera. Stock up, create, and keep a well-stocked library. Even if we never have a crisis, the knowledge found in books may provide you with the greatest return on investment you can ever have.

KITS

In addition to keeping extra food and other basic supplies around, one of the best places to start is to get at least a 72-hour survival kit. You can purchase them for $30 to $120. In my family we made our own.

A typical survival kit would include:

- Food (nonperishables) for one person for 72 hours
- Water for one person for 72 hours
- Small first aid kit with manual
- Flashlight with extra batteries
- Emergency blanket
- Notepad and pencil

One of your family's kits should also include a radio with batteries, and a tarp for emergency shelter.

Our family got together, we rounded up all the stuff, and we created a 72-hour survival kit for each member of the family. Each one fits in a half gallon container.

You can go to any of these survival type conventions that come through town and buy a survival kit to support you for 72 hours. Isn't it more likely that you'd have to deal with your electricity shutting off for a short period of time due to a tornado or flood than encounter one of these major global catastrophes like Y2K?

I remember when I got caught in the middle of Hurricane Hugo back in North Carolina. All of a sudden the windows were blowing out of the hotel. I ended up at a friend's house; we got trapped in this neighborhood for three days. His wife was a flight attendant. I was there watching the trees fall down, and guys were taking out chain saws and cutting through them. It was an amazing thing.

You know what? We made it through that very easily, but it scared me to death how fast things turned around. Your jobs can be upset just because trees are down in your driveway and you can't get out. We can't move without our cars. So first, get your 72-hour survival kit, and then start working on the food and equipment supply. Ideally you could store enough to last for one year.

2. FUEL

From wood to propane to wood pellets, every area of the country has it's own system for cooking and keeping your family warm in case of an emergency. I have a wife who particularly likes to be warm. Anything under 80 degrees is cold. So, I have to take that into account when we lose power. How important is keeping a family warm? Now, let me tell you what I did.

I put in a big generator at my house that uses propane. We have enough propane in there to last nigh one year, and it will heat and do electric work for about 60% of the house. Was it expensive? Yes. We could have purchased a cheaper version for less, but now every essential thing in the house can run. So right now, I am set. I could go, if all the electricity were shut off, gas and everything, for one year.

I suggest everybody try to do the same. Now, a typical house could be set up for between $6,000 and $15,000 (to get the deluxe model). You would have a generator that will last for three days or as long as you want it to go, depending on the amount of fuel you have stored up.

3. MONEY/SOMETHING TO EXCHANGE

Gold is a medium of exchange. Always has been, always will be. In any form, gold has been a medium of exchange. Nobody can predict how much gold would be worth if there was a nationwide catastrophe.

We saw after the First World War the German mark just shot up to where it took literally a wheelbarrow full of paper currency to buy a loaf of bread. Could that happen again? I don't think it will, but could it, in theory? Yes. That's what you need to watch out for.

Our paper money is not backed up by any gold or silver reserves at all. There is no tie between the paper money in your wallet right now to any standard of gold or silver. It is only backed up by the U.S. government. If something were to happen, then the paper currency would become virtually worthless. And then what are you going to do? What will you use as a medium of exchange? What will you use to get by?

It doesn't take Y2K or any other bugaboo to convince me or to frighten me to the point that I feel a need to be out buying gold. I have been out buying gold for the last 14 years.

You know, you could have green stuff stashed away, and I suggest that, too. Have some good old American dollars, but you should also have your gold. Once again I suggest buying the one-ounce gold coins, and silver in the smaller denominations. But you need a medium of exchange.

You also need to develop your own skills. You may be really good at the stock market, but you also may need to be a carpenter or a schoolteacher. From sheet metal to sheetrock, develop some skills that are marketable. You never know when you will need to have to trade your time in exchange for money or food.

I don't care how old you are. I don't care how skinny or overweight you are. There may be a time in your life when you need to go out and earn a living.

I know a lot of people that come to my stock market seminars who think they're doing great earning a living because they are spending 30 minutes to an hour and a half a day looking at computer screens, and buying a few options here and there. They are losing all their tradable skills, because they are developing and maintaining other skills. Be careful that you develop and maintain really good solid marketable skills.

It comes down to having something to trade. Whether you trade gold or paper money or your time, you need something to trade that will keep its value, even in a catastrophe.

4. AVOID DEBT

My strongest recommendation to help you prepare for any kind of a downturn in the economy, or specifically a downturn in your own personal economy, is to get out of debt. If you have credit cards that you use for convenience sake, fine. But if you cannot pay off the bill every month, you should not be using your credit card. Do not, do not, *do not* incur and build up consumer debt (see Chapter 11).

5. RELATIONSHIP WITH GOD

Point number five is by far the most important point. If you really want protection against a downturn in your own life, you need to develop a better relationship with God. I know that sounds cliché and you're probably saying, "Of course we should do that."

In New Testament times, the apostle Peter was walking down the street when he passed a lame person sitting by the road. Peter looked at this person and said, "Gold and silver have I none, but such as I have I give thee. In the name of Jesus of Nazareth, rise up and walk." He put out his hand and, taking the man's hands, pulled him up. Peter's words were powerful and his action was powerful. There are things out there more powerful than gold.

My strongest advice to you is this: What will help you get through catastrophes is a good, loving, caring family and your relationship with your God. You need to be praying and developing that relationship. I hope you buy some of my books such as

Business Buy The Bible, Don't Set Goals, or *A+*. I think they will help you keep on track. But much more important than buying my books is to buy a good Bible.

> *Death is not to the Christian what has often been called, "Paying the debt of nature;" it is rather bringing a note to the bank to obtain solid gold for it.—You bring a cumbrous body which is nothing worth, and lay it down, and receive for it, from the eternal treasures, liberty, victory, knowledge, and rapture.*
>
> —John Foster

I started off this book with this one thing—I see so much negativism carrying the day. Just because the economy goes into a depression, it doesn't mean that you need to go into a depression. Just because a few companies in the economy are faltering and having a hard time does not mean that you need to falter and have a hard time. Just because the American government has taken us off the gold standard does not mean that you need to go off the gold standard. That's why this relationship with you and God is so important. All of your other relationships may fail you.

The relationship you have as a citizen with the government may fail you at some time, but your relationship with God will not fail you. So what's your attitude going to be? You get to choose your course.

Be very, very careful to whom you're listening, where you are going for your advice. Keep gold in perspective. Gold is not the answer-all, catch-all, and end-all to the Y2K problem. It is a part of your portfolio. Knowledge, skills, your family and your relationship with God are a lot more important than having a few more gold coins so you can get over December 31, 1999.

10 POWERFUL INFORMATION

One of the privileges I've had is to interview James Stevens, the remarkable author I mentioned in the previous chapter. We've transcribed the interview and included it here. This is powerful information.

If you're concerned about your life, if you're concerned about taking care of your family, the author who we have in the studio now is James Stevens. He has written a book called *Making the Best of Basics*. It's a family preparedness book. It's not like a food storage or a food book. It is a whole book on the basics of family preparedness. I know that to some of you that may sound a little boring, but listen up because there's some valuable information coming and I think you all will benefit.

Wade: James, welcome.

James: Thank you. Delighted to be here.

Wade: Now what is it that drives you, and why did you write this book?

James: I wrote the book from an experiential basis. I was raised always being prepared because I lived on a farm. We always had everything. I was somewhat along in my youth before I figured out how it all got there. It didn't just happen. It took a lot of effort. I learned early on that there are no emergencies for those who are prepared. And so I've written a book to help people to be prepared for whatever.

Wade: Like what? Give me an example. What are the things they need to be concerned about?

James: There are only three things for which one needs be prepared. First, natural disasters. We can't control those. They come and we either are prepared for them, we respond or we react. The second type of disasters are the man-caused ones. Downsizing is the byword of today.

Wade: Right, being laid off.

James: Being laid off, companies closing their doors.

Wade: There could be a strike, a trucking strike.

James: A trucking strike, civil disobedience—we have a number of those incidents. Or political or whatever kind of failure that happens. It's happening all over the world. And the third kind are the personal ones. I guess interestingly enough, the first two generally cause the last one. So there's a ripple effect.

Wade: Like what? Sickness?

James: Every morning, every day there's a potential to have some kind of personal disaster. Whether it's a freeway accident, an act of vandalism against you, commuting problem, or job loss. Those things impact you personally. A company doesn't have to close for it to be a man-caused situation.

Wade: So how does your book address those three things?

James: It helps you be able to respond instead of react by being prepared. Teach people really how to have a paradigm shift as Steve Covey would say, to the concept of having a virtual convenience store in the home. Today, I wish I called the book *Back to the Pantry*, it would probably have been less mundane in today's world when everybody is "basic," including Chevrolet when they say, "Here's our five-door station wagon, it's a basic tool." That's pushing it a little bit far in my opinion. Basics is having the ability to live in a near-normal manner in a disaster situation, or when external conditions are out of your personal control.

Wade: Okay, *Making the Best of Basics*. What do you do on a daily basis? I mean, you're out promoting the book, but what do you do to get the word out?

James: Oh, I talk to people. I have lots of dealers, I go to shows, I do radio interviews. I talk to individuals who call up and question…

Wade: When you do radio shows and you go out to these expositions or these shows, are you answering the same questions over and over again?

James: Every day.

Wade: Are there a lot of skeptics? Oh what are these disasters that everybody's talking about? These guys are just out here trying to sell their books, his book is $19.95. He can't get rich off of a $19.95 book.

James: Absolutely not. If so, I wouldn't have to do all these radio shows. The important thing about the book is that it's knowledge. Knowledge is not power.

Wade: This is a big book though, James.

James: It is 336 pages long, it's 8 $1/2$ x 11 and it's two pounds!

Wade: Yes, I know, but a lot of people don't put a lot of ink on those pages. This book is full of forms and documents and everything that people need to be prepared.

James: Every page has something that I've learned the hard way.

Wade: I mean, I've thumbed through it and I could not believe it. I said, "Every page here, every paragraph on every page is worth the price of this book." There is so much valuable information.

James: Thanks for that. I hope that it is because it's taken me many years. I've lived it, every day we utilize our food storage, we put food away.

Wade: You mentioned to me on the radio show yesterday that you're using your retirement to do this. Your money, you've actually dipped into your own retirement money to print the book and to do this.

James: All of it. All of it.

Wade: All of it? Not just some of it you hear, but all of it.

James: Not some of it, all of it. And it's the most rewarding thing we've done. I'm truly enjoying it. I used to sell life insurance, and now I'm selling life assurance.

Wade: I see.

James: If I could just get them to understand that we must be prepared for whatever. And I'm not naming the disaster that's going to cause their need. The greatest fear for the prepared are those who are not, because they are going to lean on us. They're going to come to us for help.

Wade: Part of your preparedness then is food. I mean, it is food, right?

James: You gotta eat!

Wade: You gotta eat. I mean, I teach gold seminars and stock market seminars, and I say that if I had one thing, if there's a disaster, if there was one thing that I wanted; everybody says, "Gold." You know, like as a medium of exchange, and I say, "No. Food."

James: Absolutely.

Wade: If you have the gold, you can trade for food, but what you're going to need is food.

James: Food is spoken in every language.

Wade: But there are so many people that have heard about food storage and food preparedness type things before, but they think that after five or ten years their food is going to be all rotten and stale. You're not saying that at all, right? You're saying to use it?

James: I'm saying there are three rules to being prepared with food. That is, store what you eat, eat what you store and use it or you lose it. Every day, every meal we use some of our food storage so it's in constant rotation.

Wade: Well, I think that's the process here. I think that people that just get some wheat or get canned food and store it away, if they aren't even prepared on how to use it, then what good is it going to do in a crisis?

James: Well, we live in an instant gratification world. Everybody is used to going to the corner store to get their lunch, their dinner, their breakfast anymore. Families don't sit together and eat, they don't spend time together. They're not prepared to even be a family much less to be prepared to live as a family during a crisis. And I think the important thing is we must learn again how to prepare. In fact, the pantry now belongs to the corner convenience store or the all-night grocery store. Most of us don't even know how to inventory a week's supply. Get ready for a picnic for heaven's sake, much less for a year.

Wade: Now, you've updated this book a lot, correct?

James: This is in its 10th edition. Yes, it started 23 years ago.

Wade: And you've sold hundreds of thousands of copies.

James: Fortunately, yes.

Wade: Yes, I mean you've sold a lot.

James: Never had a copy come back, ever. Not even damaged copy.

Wade: Wow, that's amazing! Everyone, I think you need this book. It's called *Making the Best of Basics*, the last name is Stevens, S-T-E-V-E-N-S. It is in better bookstores everywhere. James Stevens, *Making the Best of Basics*, the family preparedness handbook. James, thanks for being here today.

James: My pleasure, thanks.

Note: James Stevens new book, Don't Get Caught With Your Pantry Down, *is also in bookstores.*

I have discovered the philosopher's stone, that
turns everything into gold: it is, "Pay as you go."
—John Randolph

11 GET OUT OF DEBT

My strongest recommendation to prepare you for any kind of a downturn in the economy, or specifically a downturn in your own economy, is to get out of debt.

I'm going to specifically talk to the young people for a minute. When I say young, I mean 18 to 25 year olds that get their first credit card, and other young people who get married.

All of a sudden, they're bombarded with these applications for credit cards with $500+ credit limits. From JC Penneys to Sears, from MasterCard/Visa to American Express, and all of a sudden they have the ability to go out and charge things.

They may live in a house that is half-barren, half full of hand-me-down furniture. The easiest thing to do is to run out and charge up a bunch of furniture, and a whole mess of expensive items with virtually no way to pay it all back. They look at $12 monthly minimum payments and think, "No problem." But all of a sudden they've got four and five and ten credit cards, and those monthly minimums become more and more.

Then they miss one and there's a $20 late charge on the next statement. Then, all of a sudden, people are in debt $5,000 to $9,000, and filing for bankruptcy.

Do you know that last year we had something like 1.3 million people in America file for bankruptcy?

How do they get into that kind of trouble? Virtually every time it was credit cards and other consumer debt. I am not going to tell you to get all your credit cards out of your wallet and cut them up. If that's what you need to discipline yourself, then go ahead, but I think it's sad to do that to discipline yourself.

You need to find out where your heart really is in all this and find out how much credit and how much debt you can handle. Here's a good rule of thumb: If you can't pay it off at the end of the month, don't buy it. Use credit cards only for convenience, not for spreading out payments.

Here's the problem: We live in a high debt society. You can get anything you want on credit. Look at the television at nighttime and you can get your whole house re-carpeted on credit. You won't even have any payments or interest for the next 15 months! So, you get your house re-carpeted and you're only $6,000 or $7,000 in debt. By the way, did you know that if you're willing to pay cash you could have done the whole thing for $3,000?

In no time, there's an additional commitment here and another commitment there. Pretty soon people get so strapped, they put themselves in a bad situation if any crisis comes.

Get out of debt! Stay out of debt!

WHAT ABOUT YOUR OWN HOME?

Should you pay off your own house? Is this kind of debt okay?

Strategic business or investment debt is about the only type of debt that I would agree to. Falling within that category would be buying your own home. Let me tell you why I think that buying your own home is an okay form of debt.

It is simple. In almost every situation, the house is worth more than the debt. If you buy a house that's worth $180,000, you may get a $150,000 loan. You come up with a $30,000 down payment. You're paying off the $150,000 over the next 25 to 30 years. Make sure that the payment is affordable. If it's too high, that can cause additional problems.

Please take this next thing I'm going to say to heart. If both the husband and the wife have to work in order to afford the mortgage payment, you are probably in too much debt. I've been doing financial seminars for a number of years and it is amazing to me how many people with full, good intentions, and with husband and wife both working, get involved in a $2,000 to $4,000 monthly payment on a house. They both have to work to afford it.

A young couple with just the husband (or one spouse) working should try to buy as big a house with as high a mortgage as they can afford. That sounds crazy, but read on. I remember my parents back in the 1950s were buying a house for $8,000.

"But honey!" I remember my mom saying (I was very young, and I remember being into financial things even at the age of seven and eight years old).

I remember my mom and dad talking, "This is $90 a month! Do you think we can get them to lower the interest rate down to 4% instead of 4.5%?"

It sounds like a fictitious thing that I'm saying, does it not?

How many of you have parents that were in similar situations—that have had houses they purchased at $8,000 to $10,000 with really low payments decades ago? You know what? That $80 or $90 at the first part of a new 30-year mortgage was an awesome, huge amount of money. Just like $1,500 a month may be to somebody today.

With inflation and other factors, $1,500 today, may, in 30 years, increase a house payment to $9,000 a month! Your $1,500 a month payment is going to be talked about by your kids. "Yes, my mom and dad have it made! Their payment is only $1,500!"

They aren't aware of what you had to struggle with for 20 or 30 years to get it to the point that $1,500 compared to $6,000 to $9,000 is a small amount of money.

So let me say it again. To the extent that you can afford it *with one person working,* get as big a mortgage as you possibly can. And then go to work at paying it off.

HOW TO PAY OFF YOUR MORTGAGE

Now, I'm going to tell you briefly how to do just that, but I recommend you read my book called **Business Buy The Bible**. In the back of that book, there is an appendix with a specific plan for how to pay off your mortgage. However, I'll explain it here in general.

If you have a house payment of $1,200, out of $1,200 you have $100 for principal and $1,100 toward interest. When you pay that house payment of $1,200, send in one extra principal payment every month. At first, it's not very much. It's $100, and then increases to $101, so you send in $1,301 instead of $1,200. That extra principal payment every month will pay off your mortgage in record time.

With a 30-year mortgage, there are 30 years of interest payments and 30 years of principal payments. If you pay one extra principal payment a month, you will pay off a 30-year mortgage in 15 years. What if you pay two extra principal payments a month? Let's stick with that for moment.

Two at the very beginning of the life of a mortgage may be affordable, but two principal payments later on when the principal part of the payment is huge and the interest part is small, when the loan balance gets low, may be difficult to do.

But right now, at the beginning of your mortgage, when you can make a little extra principal payment, do so. If you make two extra principal payments, you will pay off a 30-year mortgage in 10 years. If you make three extra principal payments, you'll pay off a 30-year mortgage in seven and a half years. If you make four extra principal payments, you'll pay off a 30-year mortgage in six years. It's easy. Just take the one that you must make plus four; that's five principal payments total. Divide five principal payments into thirty years, and the result is six years.

Now you have taken a 30-year mortgage and paid it off in seven and a half years. Tell me how you're going to feel when you do not have a house payment. Has anybody ever had that experience before? It is the most awesome feeling to not have a house payment.

I bought a very expensive home and farm (actually a partnership bought it and we're the caretakers). Now let me tell you what happened. I ganged up on the payments. I worked extra hard. I said to my wife, "Look, if I make this commitment to do this, there is a price to pay. We both need to step up to the plate. This will take a huge amount of work on my part to do this."

She said, "Wade, I don't want you to get a hernia over this."

I said, "I'm willing to pay this price to get it paid off within two years."

Now I want to tell you something. I have experienced something extra when I was dedicated to erasing debt. If you make the commitment to get and stay out of debt, it is as if the very forces of nature will get out of your way, and lay down before you to allow you to accomplish your mission. The most awesome things happened through that two years. I was able to take in $140,000 on the 23rd month and pay off a multimillion dollar house in 23 months. I made it one month early.

Now, if I had not had the dedication to pay it off, I guarantee you, I'd be making payments for 28 years. You literally have got to say, "I am going to pay off this debt. I am going to take every bonus check I get from work and put it toward the principal on my house! I'm going to work extra hard, and I'm going to get a raise and when I get that raise, that extra money is going against the principal on my house!" If you have that kind of dedication, then incredible things will happen.

Get out of debt, not only in preparation of possible future events, but because of the personal advantages that having no debt can provide. And believe me, the advantages are significant.

12 GOLD MINING COMPANIES

Another way to invest in gold is to invest in companies that mine and process gold. I want to show you a chart. This chart is placed here so you can see the price of gold at various times. Quite dramatic moves, don't you agree? I think everybody should pay some attention to gold charts like these.

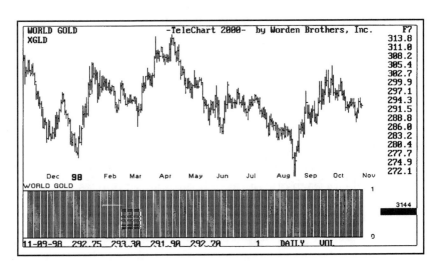

Now, you can see that gold has been way up. It was around $340. Gold dropped a lot, but then it has gone up and down, and it is back up right now to around $300. It dipped clear down to $280, even $276.

You might also want to own stocks in these companies. It's just another gold play. If you can buy these stocks on dips, it may be a way to increase your portfolio. When gold is down, these stocks are down. Buy low, sell high.

THE COST OF GOLD

One of the reasons gold stocks have been down, is because to mine gold and get it to the point where it is marketable requires a number of dollars.

Let's get specific. Let's say that a few years ago when gold was up around $400 per ounce, it cost $280 an ounce to mine. That's a nice profit.

There are barges on rivers in Northern California that go up and down and pan for gold. There are other places that have huge digging equipment where they go down into tunnels and caves for mining gold. There are strip mines: they take off layer after layer of the dirt, and keep finding gold. There are many, many different ways of finding gold, but most of them require machinery and people to operate them. In our example, all the costs of mining one ounce totals to about $280.

These companies obviously are looking for more than just one ounce. They mine hundreds of ounces a day and thousands of ounces per year. The cost per ounce comes out to about $280 in our example for each one of those thousands of ounces.

Well, as long as gold is at $380 and $400, there's a nice profit. They can mine the gold, hold it in their account, and then sell it. If they think gold is on a dip, say from $380 down to $360, they can wait. "It's just a temporary thing. The price is going to go back up," and the gold company that is doing the mining can hold it and sell it at a more opportune time.

What if gold costs $280 an ounce to mine and they have to sell it for $290? The margins are now too thin. What happens if the cost of retrieving gold—the cost of mining it, manufacturing it, and refining—gets more expensive than the price they can get on the market by selling it? Do they keep going? Do you keep mining it? Should they keep losing money on current operations?

Some companies say, "Yes, we keep doing that because as gold goes back up, even though it costs a little bit more today to mine it, it will be worth more in a year or two." This company is gambling on the future that gold prices will go back up. Some hedge by selling future gold but lock in the price today.

These companies are out mining and manufacturing gold to make a profit. I am in the seminar business and my company has investments in hotels and various properties. We build a hotel and we have debt on it. Then we try to rent out the rooms as a way to make profit on the business. So, we're buying and selling, buying and selling. Gold mining companies are doing the same thing.

Some companies, and this is public information, literally state in their SEC report the cost to get an ounce of gold out of the ground. If you want to know what the current figure is, go look at the financial reports of a few gold companies.

Some gold is very easy to get. Have you ever heard the expression "placer?" Placer is a type of gold that is easy to mine. It is actually gold that doesn't need to be mined at all.

The definition of placer is a deposit of sand or gravel containing particles of value or minerals such as gold. So placer gold is gold that is really easy to mine. They can mine placer gold, which is hard to find, but they can mine it for $180 to $200 an ounce. My goodness, they can obtain an even larger profit at that amount.

But if they have to strip mine, bring in a lot of equipment, or go out into rivers and dredge, it is very costly to mine gold. Recently, for some companies, the market price of gold is the same price they would get if they were to mine it. There's just not a lot of profits lately. Hence, gold stocks have gone down.

I don't want to get too technical, but there has arisen another problem with gold stocks. Most of you probably don't know what "hedging your bet" is in regards to gold. We do it all the time.

Let's say a gold company has a lot of gold reserves, and is actively mining their gold at such and such a price. They don't believe that gold prices are going to be sustained. This company could take some of its profits from selling gold, go out and buy or sell futures, or buy puts on gold, and be hedged against any movement in the gold price.

There are other companies that are called completely unhedged companies. They have none of their cash tied up in securities positions; all of their money is tied up in gold reserves. That's my recommendation by the way. I don't want to buy stock in a bunch of companies that are playing all kinds of securities markets, trying to gamble which way the gold price is going to go. I want a company that's paying attention to its Ps and Qs and is mining gold out of the ground or out of rivers at a very, very inexpensive price.

Let me say that again. This is a very important statement. I want to invest in companies that are getting better at the mining process, and are keeping their cost of extracting and mining gold to a really, really small price.

SAMPLING OF GOLD MINING COMPANIES

Note: I give no recommendation to buy or sell. This is for educational purposes only. And, think, anything I write here may be outdated by the time this book is published and you read this.

This information is a snapshot in time. Please do your own research for the timeliness and appropriateness of your investment.

SOME COMPANIES TO PERUSE

Echo Bay Mine, ticker symbol ECO.

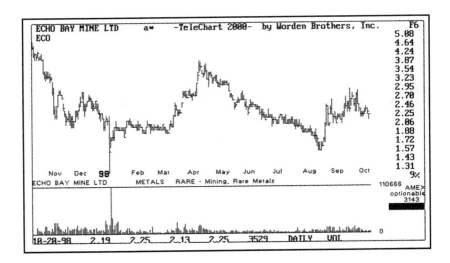

You see here gold going up again earlier this year. The price for this stock went down. By the way, this stock was up around $5 a share, it tumbled down to around $2, climbed back up to around $3.50, and then went back down.

Could a gold stock turn into a rolling stock? Very easily! As gold prices go up, the stock price goes up. As gold prices go down, the stock price goes down.

I have rolled Royal Oak Mines, ticker symbol RYO, I have rolled Amex Gold, the old ticker symbol is AU, which ironically is a cool ticker symbol, is it not? AU for gold, because AU is also the element symbol for gold. Now that company has been folded into another company, I think it used to be called Amex Gold and the ticker was AU. They roll! I roll a lot of these. I rolled one from $5 to $7, I rolled another one from $2.50 to $3.50, that was Royal Oak Mines and that's a little bit under that right now.

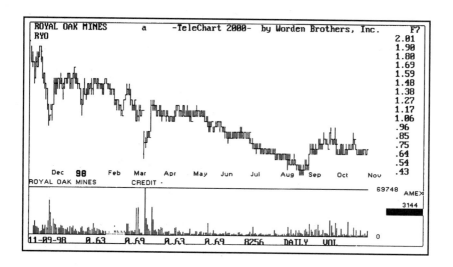

Look at this one. This is Battle Mountain Gold, and has been one of my favorites, ticker symbol is BMG.

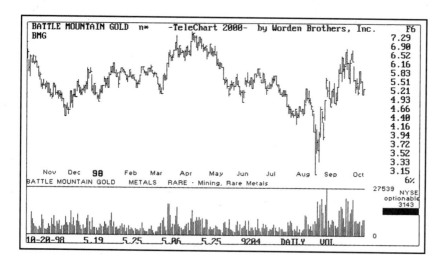

Look at this roll here. Through this last year, the stock gets down around $5, and then it rolls up around $6.25. Placer Dome, the one I just talked about, PDG is the ticker symbol.

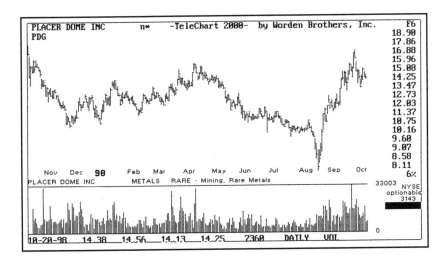

By the way, earlier, I think last year, the stock was like $25 to $28 a share. It is down now around $13 to $14 and look at the nice roll.

Now, I'm not saying you should be investing in these as Rolling Stocks, I'm saying that the stocks are weak right now. Why? Simply because gold prices are down.

Now, compare this, if you will, in your mind to that gold chart where gold kept getting around $280 and it would bounce back up. Every time gold goes down to around $280 and then bounces back up, gold stocks are down at that same time. What is probably going to happen as gold prices go back up? What's going to happen to the price of those gold stocks? They are going to go back up. So, if you want to play the quick turn game and learn how to make some money, this is a way to do it.

Another stock is Barrick Gold, another great company.

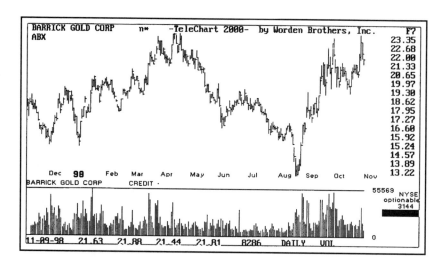

The stock was up around the $20 to $30 range, and has just gone up, come down and is currently around $20.

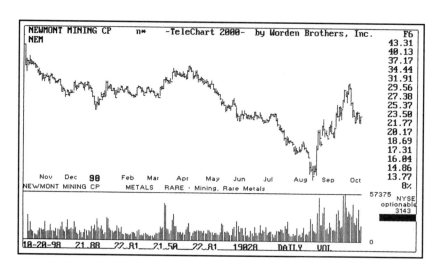

Another huge company, this one gets a lot of attention, Newmount Mining, NEM is the ticker symbol. A lot of people follow this stock.

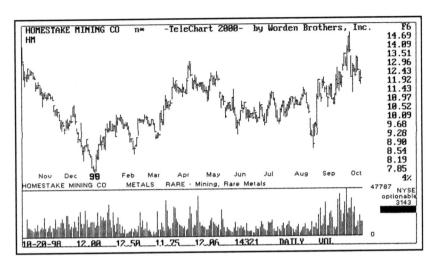

Homestake Mining is another that I've been investing in over the last several years. By the way, I was able to get some of this at $8 and $9 a share way back. It's currently up around $12 to $15 a share.

A TRICK OF MAGIC

I want to show you something rather fun and I hope you can just stick with me on this. The first time I did this was with transparencies that I put up with a very bright light so that you could seem them easily. The effect in print is not quite as dramatic.

I'm going to take six charts of six different companies that I just showed you, and put them here together.

Now you are looking at six charts superimposed over one another (on next page). Some of those lines representing different dollar amounts from different companies create a very similar pattern. Review and take a look at all six of these charts previously in this chapter. Can you see some distinct patterns? You see that they are almost all doing the same thing at the same time.

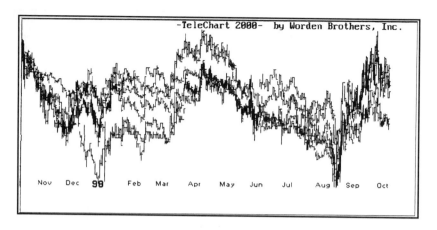

One of the things this tells me, if I'm going to get good at this, is if I've got an $8 stock that goes to $10, it's a nice move. But, if at the same time another company has a $1 stock going to $2, even though it's only a $1 move, would you rather make a $1 profit on a $1 stock or a $2 profit on a $8 stock? See the point?

Study gold mining stocks. There are 30 to 50 companies that mine gold. Some of them are just gold companies and some of them also mine copper and other things as well. It's good to do your research.

Again, in the gold index chart from (page 87), you can see a nice roll pattern. With this information, you can buy gold when it's low, sell it when it's high, and maybe make a little bit of money. Or, you can just buy it for the long term. Keep buying it on dips.

If you're really buying gold for the next 5 to 15 years, and that's what I think you should be doing, and if you look at this pattern, when would you buy gold? If you're going to buy it for the long term, would you rather be paying $280 or wait for it to get to $310 and then buy. See the point? It's facetious. So now that you know this, buy it on dips.

I PROMISES OF VALUE

t about the time this book was ready to go to press, in the late fall of 1998, a few prominent people made comments on gold. They were not only timely, but their statements contained underlying promises of lasting value. I've included a few here.

Steve Forbes, the editor-in-chief of *Forbes Magazine*, is a man I respect. His financial insights, both of a domestic nature and internationally, are well thought out and on target.

Commenting on his editorial page in the November 2, 1998 edition, page 31, he said, "The Federal Reserve inadvertent tight money policy has deepened the global deflation, sending commodity prices crashing across the board. The Fed has not yet grasped the fact that the dollar is an international currency. Greenspan & Company must aggressively pump out new liquidity so that the price of gold will once again reach the level of $350. When will Washington wake up to what needs to be done—and then do it?"

Walter Rauleau in his *Growth Fund Guide* asked the question: "Is gold undervalued relative to the U.S. stock market?" His answer: "When you look at gold's relative valuation to the S&P 500, you can get that it is more undervalued than it has ever been in the last 100 years. In 1980, gold was a hot item that most investors wanted to own; at the time, it was selling for six times the value of the S&P 500. Recently, you could have bought an ounce of gold bullion for less 1/4 the price of the S&P 500. So, on a historical relative value basis, we believe that gold is cheap. And we believe it is likely to be at the early portion of a new bull market."

I heartily agree. However, defining the major correction of 1998 as a bear market (so a bull market can begin) is controversial. If, technically, you want to call it a bear market, it is the shortest one in history. See my book *Bulls and Bears* (formerly titled *Bear Market Baloney*).

II WEALTH 101

The following information is excerpted from *Wealth 101*, my new best-selling book. It briefly gives you the information to further protect yourself through entity structuring. For more information on seminars, books, and home study courses, call 1-800-872-7411. To set up one of these entities, call Entity Planners, Inc. at 1-800-706-4741.

DIVIDE AND CONQUER

The whole thrust of protecting assets is to divide and conquer. Make sure that you do not make all of your money in one legal entity, and that you do not hold all your assets or have your income made by one entity. Basically, there are three different Goliaths out there. One of the things that can jump up and bite you in the fanny is a lawsuit. The second one is income taxes, which can seriously curtail what you're trying to do. The third one is death taxes.

Now, think about these three again: lawsuits, income taxes, and death taxes. If you make all the money you're going to make under your own name, and if all the assets you hold are held under your own name, then you stand pretty vulnerable. Think about that. Can one lawsuit then wipe out everything? Can having just one income tax bracket for everything minimize your money?

The answer to all three financial problems is to split up your assets to make sure that you do not own all of your things in one legal entity. Let's go through all of these in detail. As we go through them, you'll hear a lot about these different entities. If you need more information or forms and documents, once again I'll refer you to the available resources in Appendix III, which lists all of the ways we can furnish that information to you.

What we're trying to do is to make sure that you have a lot of money set aside for your retirement, and that as you're growing your assets, you grow as rapidly as possible by keeping the chips on your side of the table. If you have a business that could bring about different risks and exposure levels, you protect the other business enterprises you have.

If I were to own three rental properties, I wouldn't want to own those in one corporation or one limited partnership. If I bought a Chinese restaurant I would want that in a separate, distinct corporation. If I had a 20 unit apartment building I'd want that in yet a different limited partnership.

I have different tax vehicles. I have them isolated away from each other. Somebody coming into my Chinese restaurant corporation and suing would affect that corporation. That corporation may even have to go bankrupt, but it would not affect the other corporations and it would not affect me personally. So the thrust behind this whole concept is to divide and conquer.

A CORPORATION

This strategy is about the importance of having a corporation. We're not talking about a Nevada Corporation yet. We're just talking about a regular corporation. I'm going to give you a list of reasons why I think corporations are good.

The number one reason why corporations are so powerful, and the workhorse of this whole business enterprise is simply because the alternatives are not very good. Sole proprietorships, in particular, should be outlawed in my opinion.

Let me tell you what I do on a day-to-day basis. We have a staff of 30 to 45 people that consult with people all over the country. We help people set up their corporations and their limited partnerships. We help people decide on real estate transactions, on which ones they're going to do and not going to do, and how much money they are going to make, et cetera. That's what we do.

Now, every day we get incredibly great phone calls from people who are making money. But most of the phone calls coming in aren't about the good stuff. They are about the bad stuff. By the way, we only do consulting three or four hours a day because that's about all our staff can handle. We don't like all these negative things, and almost all the negative things happen because people did not take time to set themselves up legally and structure themselves.

People call on the phone and they say, "I went to your seminar eight years ago. It was wonderful. I loved it. I went out and made all this money, and now I'm getting sued," or, "Wade, I should have listened to you a long time ago. I went out and did it. I made a whole bunch of money, but now I'm getting killed on taxes, 40% of what I make is going to the government."

Had people taken time out to do it right, to get financially fit for the opportunity, then they wouldn't be having all these problems. And again, the number one entity, the one that everybody needs is a corporation. Of all the people I've met—the tens of thousands of people I've met—every one has needed a corporation. Most people need two or three corporations, or perhaps four or five to handle their different investments. They at least need one or two corporations for moving money from one state to another. They need corporations to have different tax brackets. They need to have corporations to protect their riches for their children to use for college, and to retire on later. There's so much that can be done with a corporation, and in a lot of ways corporations are light years ahead of a Living Trust for estate planning purposes. A Living Trust avoids probate, but a corporation allows all kinds of things.

Now for my list of reasons why I think corporations are so great:

1. Sole proprietorships are so bad. You go to these attorneys and they tell you to go ahead and be a sole proprietorship because you're not big enough to be a corporation. Well, now you have no tax planning vehicle at all. You have no lessening of your exposure to risk in liability. You have no ability to move money off from one year to another. You just minimized everything that you could do by doing it as a sole proprietorship.

2. If you're ever going to do personal investments or run a business, the corporation helps you divide up your income and your assets into different legal entities, thereby lessening the risk of loss.

3. The risk or the exposure to liability by the officers, directors, and the shareholders, in most instances, is seriously reduced or eliminated by a corporation. You, as shareholder of your own little family corporation, are not liable for the activities of the corporation. As an officer, if you do something illegal then you may be held liable.

   If you run a corporation right, you set it up and you do it right, it takes title to businesses, it takes title to real estate or whatever, and if it's running and operating the right way and the books are accurate, then there's no way that somebody can go through the corporation and sue you. I know these attorneys talk about piercing the corporate veil, and I challenge them all the time to find me one case where it's happened. So far, no one has done it; that's just attorney talk. And, by the way, what's the alternative?

4. Corporations are eternal, they're perpetual in nature. Some of you right now are going to be setting up corporations that will be around 200 and 300 years from now. They'll support your kids, your grandkids, and your great grandkids in these businesses and enterprises that you're getting into. The corporation will outlive you.

5. From an estate planning point of view, corporations are phenomenal. They allow you to divide the stock in any way you choose to your kids and grandkids. You can have voting stock and nonvoting stock, and you as the parents keep the voting stock. You can have preferred stock and common stock.

You can divide small amounts to the parents in a corporation that's just getting started, and give huge amounts of stock to the kids. There's no tax consequence, because the stock is not really worth anything at the very beginning. When you put money into the corporation, you can loan it to the corporation, so that you can get the money back in a year or two as a loan repayment and have no tax consequences. I could go on and on, but I think you get the point. If you need more corporate information, give us a call at 1-800-872-7411.

CHOOSE A NEVADA CORPORATION

Choose a Nevada Corporation. I just cannot stress the importance of this. It doesn't matter what state you are in, you should set up a Nevada Corporation. Why Nevada? Because in Nevada there's no corporate income tax, no stock transfer tax, no franchise tax, and no succession tax.

Don't get me wrong here. If you do business in one state and you make a profit in that state, you will have to pay some business taxes on the profits there, but you will not have to pay taxes on money you make in other states. You will not have to pay taxes on money that you make on a national basis, like your investments.

For example, you could have a California company, but do that as a Nevada Corporation. Now, that Nevada Corporation could also have a brokerage account at Charles Schwab, or whatever, in Las Vegas so that none of those dividends or capital gains are being taxed in the State of California.

If you do business in California they tax you on any money you make in that state, any other state, in any other country in the world. California acts like a state in and of itself and not as a part of the United States of America. Several other states are moving in that direction. Taxes are a big reason, but everybody wants to make them the only reason. I think it's about 20% of the reason why you should be a Nevada Corporation.

In Nevada, the officers of a corporation cannot be sued for the activities of the corporation. These officers could be you and your wife, or you and a couple of friends that have set up a corporation. In Nevada, they simply legislated it out of existence-the officers cannot be sued for the activities of the corporation.

Also, Nevada is a total secrecy state—no one can find out who owns the stock in your company. Nevada is the only state that has not signed an information sharing agreement with the IRS.

In Nevada, anybody can own stock in the company, which means foreigners can own stock in the company. To make a long story short, Nevada is the number one place.

Delaware used to be the number one state. By the way, in some of my books I do a side-by-side comparison of Nevada and Delaware. Delaware was the best for many, many years and it's now second best. Even if you were to compare the top two states in this country, Nevada and Delaware, Nevada would win hands down, but there really is no comparison. The list reads Nevada, Delaware, New Hampshire, Idaho, and then on down-with number 50 being California.

So no matter what state you are doing business in, you need to set up your legal structure in Nevada. If you domicile it there, you can do business in a myriad of states and you lessen a lot of exposure to risk.

We have the best company ever for setting up these Nevada Corporations. We set up a corporation with 25 million shares of stock. That's the authorized stock. We encourage you to issue a million shares. We set up the corporation in Nevada with redeemable stock so the company can buy back the stock.

Let's say, for example, one of your kids marries somebody that you don't like. You can buy back the stock at par value. So, if you've issued 200,000 shares of stock to that child, you can buy that stock back at $200 because the par value is at .001. We set it up with preferred stock and common stock, which nobody else, that I know of, does.

Right now I'm the second largest producer of Nevada Corporations in the whole country, and I'm fast approaching number one. My competitor, the one who's in first position, has been in business 13 years longer than I have. (We'll catch them this year or next and have as many corporations set up as they do because we are the very, very best.) If you want to set up a Nevada Corporation, call us at 1-800-706-4741 and we'll start all the processing there, and then send it down to our Las Vegas address where it's all handled appropriately in an efficient manner. Make sure that your corporation does for you what you really want it to do. For a free seminar cassette, call 1-800-872-7411 and ask for the "Power of Nevada Corporations."

LIVING TRUSTS

We're going to switch off the corporation. From time to time we'll come back to corporations and how they work in regard to these other legal entities and how they are integrated together. However, for this one it's just the basics of a Living Trust and what this is all about.

Has anybody noticed that Living Trust seminars are kind of a phenomena the last few years? You didn't see them seven, eight, nine, or ten years ago. It's kind of a recent phenomena. I've been teaching Living Trust seminars for over a decade. What I see is a lot of these ambulance chasing attorneys out there teaching right now. They don't get it. They understand the basics of a Living Trust, but they don't understand how limited they are and yet how wonderful they can be.

The reason that Living Trusts have really gotten popular is because of the problems of probate. Even though some states have streamlined the probate process, it is still a horrible, ugly process.

When someone dies, if they own things, in order to transfer those things from one person to another it has to go before a court. Now, I believe that a will is the most dangerous document in this country, because it lulls people into a state of complacency. People think that because they have a will everything is going to be taken care of. Nothing could be further from the truth.

All wills, 100% of them, have to go through the probate process. So having a will is just slightly better than not having a will. By the way, why do you think attorneys will write up a will for you for $50 and keep it in their safe deposit box for the next 40 years waiting for you to die? Because they want to get their claws into everything that you're about. I mean, your estate is their re-tirement vehicle—and you want to keep your estate and your af-fairs out of the hands of attorneys upon your death.

The only way to avoid probate is to not die. If you do die, there's another really, really good way that almost assures that you'll avoid the probate process—die as a pauper, then you have nothing to transfer from you or your estate to anybody else. Think that one through: you die as a pauper; you don't have anything.

You could work for and control $10 million or $100 million in assets, but none of that is in your own personal name. How do you set it up so you can do that? Well, you put everything that you own—remember that 5% of the stock in one of those corporation and 2% in another corporation that you and your wife own-you put that into a Living Trust. The trust now owns that stock.

Upon your death the trustee, whoever you choose to handle your affairs when you're not here, steps in and takes control of your company. You don't have anything in your estate, and there's no cause for probate because everything has been transferred before you die.

Well, while you're alive, we're going to set this trust up as a Living Trust, an inter vivos trust. You may want to make changes to it from time to time, so we'll set it up as a revocable trust. That is really two different trusts, which today is actually a hybrid trust of those two. Sometimes, it's referred to as a family trust, which is pretty much the same thing.

A Living Trust has two functions upon your death. One function is that it keeps everything together, those things that you want to keep together those things that will support your family and pay for your kids to go to college. The other thing that it does is to give things away, just like a will. "I give to my son the '57 Chevy, I give to my daughter the jewelry"—it gives things away.

It gives certain things away and it keeps certain things together for your family. Eventually, the Living Trust is going to end; it will disburse everything when your children get older, but a Living Trust is remarkable because it avoids probate.

Now remember the three reasons for estate planning: the first is to avoid probate, the second is to avoid or reduce estate taxes, and the third is to provide for the continuity of your assets. That's what this does. Living Trusts are great. Now let me just give you a few other items that you need to make sure of. (This is where a lot of these attorneys go wrong.)

1. A Living Trust needs to be fully funded. You need to have everything put into the Living Trust, everything you own. From now on you cease to exist. You don't have anything in your own name. When you go to the movies you're going with Living Trust money. When you buy groceries you're buying groceries with Living Trust money. Everything you do, you do as a Living Trust-this is you. The Living Trust is really you while you're alive. Now, you, as the husband and wife, are the co-trustees of this trust and you just handle your everyday affairs; just remember, it needs to be fully funded.

2. In case you forgot to put something in the Living Trust before you died, there is a document called a Joint Pour-Over Will, or a Pour-Over Will, which pours over, into the Living Trust upon your death, anything you forgot to put in the Living Trust. Is this the answer? You need this Joint Pour-Over Will, but you should never have to use it, because your Living Trust truly needs to be fully funded.

3. This is where another big gap exists in the Living Trusts prepared by most attorneys. If you use us to set up your Living Trust, we will set it up with what is called a catastrophic illness clause in case, for example, you were to get seriously ill, and have $300,000 or $400,000 in doctor bills.

If you apply for Medicaid and your financial statements show you're worth quite a bit of money they'll say, "Just sell off your assets to pay the bills." Now watch what happens: if you or your wife were to get sick, you and your wife could decide to execute this catastrophic clause. At that point in time the husband's or the wife's half of the trust becomes irrevocable; it becomes a grantor trust. Everything in that trust is now held by the trust, and it has nothing to do with the ownership of the husband or the wife at that point in time.

Let's say it's the husband that is sick. Now, his half of the Living Trust is irrevocable, and the wife's half is still a revocable Living Trust. When he goes in to apply for Medicaid and they ask him how much his house is worth, he can reply, "Zero." Again, when they ask him how much his investments are worth-zero. You see, you don't have anything. Everything is out of your name and you now qualify for full Medicaid. So, Living Trusts are really great because they can trigger certain events in the future that will still protect your assets.

4. This last one is really, really important. If you own a house in a joint tenancy as a husband and wife, which, by the way, is not quite as good as owning as tenants in common, which is nowhere near as good as owning it as a Living Trust. If you live in a community property state, a lot of the things that I'm going to show you right now are available to you. But let's talk about joint tenancy.

You own a house in joint tenancy; you bought it many, many years ago for $100,000. The house today is worth $500,000. Upon the death of the husband, the wife goes to sell the house because she doesn't want to live there anymore. She sells it for $500,000, and the IRS steps in and says they need to determine what taxes are due on the deal. They will want to know how she owned the house. It was owned in joint tenancy.

Well, we just divide the house in half. What is her basis? Her basis in the property is $50,000, or half of the $100,000 original purchase price. Then they allow her to receive basis at the time of his death. The house is worth $500,000 when he died. His basis then would have been $250,000. She sells the house for $500,000, her basis is $50,000, her husband's basis is $250,000, add those two together and you have a $300,000 basis in the property, which generates a $200,000 capital gain.

If she's older than 55, she has the $125,000 one time exclusion, but she'd still have to pay capital gains on $75,000; if she's younger than 55, she would have to pay capital gains on the whole $200,000. I know a lot of women out there that dislike the IRS more than men. They'll stay living in that house for 18 or 20 years just to spite the IRS, and not have to pay them any money. And they don't really even want to live there.

Let's do it a second way—don't own the house in joint tenancy. (By the way, I dislike joint tenancy immensely.) You own the house between the husband and wife in a Living Trust. Upon the death of the husband, the wife sells the house for $500,000 as co-trustee of the Living Trust.

In steps the IRS: they need to determine what the capital gains are. Again, they want to know how the house was owned. It was assigned in a Living Trust; the wife receives the house. How much was it worth when her husband died? It was worth $500,000. All right, she gets to receive it at the full stepped up basis, not half. The wife sells it for $500,000. The full stepped up, or new basis is $500,000, and she has zero capital gains and no taxes to pay.

These Living Trusts are really sharp. They really function well. Most of the attorneys that teach Living Trust seminars have no idea of the consequences or the tax liabilities and the tax savings afforded by a Living Trust. They're really quite remarkable. You need to have one. By the way, if the wife stays living in the house, and sells it later for $600,000, she has now established a new basis of $500,000 at the time of her husband's death. In that scenario she'd have a $100,000 capital gain.

A GREAT RETIREMENT

This one is about getting ready for a great retirement and setting up a retirement entity. You've all heard of tax free investments, like municipal bonds and some other investments that produce cash flow, tax write offs, and growth, but how would you like to have an entity set up that takes everything that you would ever get involved in-everything-and turns it all into a tax free investment?

You have a few choices. One choice is to set up an IRA. I believe that everybody should have an IRA, even if you cannot deduct the standard $2,000. You should also set up IRAs for your children, and if you have a company pay your children each $2,000 to work for your company, then put that whole $2,000 into an IRA. Think about what you just did—you got rid of $2,000 out of your company, so that's less taxes, but now the $2,000 is going into an IRA for one of your children.

The second choice is a SEP-IRA-Simplified Employee Pension IRA. If you're self-employed or a sole proprietorship, you can sock aside up to $30,000 into a SEP-IRA. If you're self-employed you can also set up a more elaborate Keogh plan. I like a Keogh plan for a sole proprietorship, and/or a corporate Pension Plan if you are a corporation.

The plan that gives you the maximum strength, maximum protection, and maximum power is a corporate pension, and there are many, many reasons for doing that. I love corporations because they can take advantage of having this great Pension Plan. You can put away up to $30,000.

Don't let your CPAs tell you it's $22,500, because they've lowered the limits on Pension Plans. Don't fall into all the garbage that's being taught out there. You have different types of plans-money purchase plans and profit sharing plans. You can put 5% in your money purchase plan and 15% in your profit sharing, that's 20%. The limits have been lowered to $150,000. Well, 20% of

$150,000 is $30,000. So you still put aside your $30,000, and, by the way, if somebody is telling you $22,500, you hang up the phone on them and you call my company. We'll help you set up your Pension Plan.

In a corporation you can set aside huge amounts of money. Based on the compensation that you're paying yourself, your wife, or any of your employees, you can put aside up to $30,000 per year per person. That's $30,000 for the husband and $30,000 for the wife. That becomes a tax write off right now; it's a donation. Because it's a sponsored plan, you get to have that as a contribution to the plan, and you get to deduct the money right now. You have a big, huge tax savings right now.

You also get to be the trustee of this plan. What does that mean? It means that you've got the checkbook. It's in your glove box, it's in your purse, it's in your pocket, and you're out writing checks.

So you set up this tax free entity, you get the tax deductions, and now you've got the checkbook. If you have a Pension Plan set up at Charles Schwab or Dean Witter or Merrill Lynch, as I've said before you're limited on what you can do. You can do their types of investments. Now, you may still be able to make a lot of money with that, especially if you do the Rolling Stock plan, but why not have the checkbook?

If you're driving down the street and you see a house that you can buy and fix up using my Money Machine style, then buy and sell the house. Make a huge amount of money, with multiple checks coming in for 25 or 30 years. You've got the checkbook. You're in control of the investments of this Pension Plan.

What I'm talking about is called a self trusteed plan, where nobody else touches your money. You keep control of your money and put your whole financial destiny into your own hands. Think about this: a lot of people ask me what a trust is, as if a trust were a thing. A trust is not a thing.

A trust is a relationship between three people. There is a trustor, that's the person that sets it up and funds it; there's the trustee, that's the person that takes care of the money; and there's the beneficiary. In most trust situations those three people are different. For example, if you want to give money to your kids, you set up a trust, you put the money into a bank, the bank takes care of the money as the trustee, and your kids get it later on. But think about this one.

In the Pension Plan I'm talking about here, who's the trustor? You are. You're the corporation that sets up the Pension Plan. Who's the trustee? You are, you've got the checkbook. And who's the beneficiary? You are. You're the trustor, the trustee and the beneficiary of the same money. It doesn't get more exciting than this, because you control all the money going in, how much you're going to put in, you control the money once it's in, and you can control the money coming out. That's pretty exciting!

A couple of quick points about this Pension Plan. Again, I've got all day seminars on Pension Plans that give you a lot more detailed information. You need to get better at the law of leverage. We set up a Pension Plan that can have a margin account. We're the only one that I know of in the whole country that sets up Pension Plans that have the availability of having a margin account, and we charge a fair amount for that. Remember, you have the checkbook, so you can put some money in this brokerage account, you could put some money over here, you could have some in CDs, whatever you want to do. You're in control of the money.

Another quick point: the money is liquid in there, which means that you can borrow against the money. Remember, you're the trustee, so you're on the loan committee and you can borrow the money. You have to borrow it for serious reasons, like medical expenses or buying a house or something like that, and you have to pay it back within five years at a fair interest rate. But you can borrow the money if you need to get at the money in the future. In your Pension Plan, it's easy to set up. It's easy to operate because we do a lot of it for you.

If you get involved with other companies that set up Pension Plans, they may get you in at dirt cheap prices. However, then you have to buy all of your investments through them, and they not only charge you their normal commissions, but sometimes they charge you pension fees on top of that. Also, if they're managing your money, they definitely charge you annual fees at the end of the year, sometimes up to 3% of your assets in the Pension Plan. We have no such fees if you use us. So be very careful on who you choose to help you with the administration of your Pension Plan. They're one of the neatest entities around, but they're also highly regulated. So you need to be very, very careful.

Now you control it, you can diversify your investments, you can put in huge amounts of money, get tax deductions right now, and the money sits there and grows tax free. When you sell your properties, all the capital gains have no consequences. All the income, investment income, interest income, dividend income-no consequences.

The entity that you should be using to get wealthy is a retirement entity. Most people have never thought about that. They're always trying to build up their company and get their company rich, or to build up their own personal net worth and get themselves rich. But why not sock aside money into a pension account and have the pension account get rich.

A lot of the strategies that I told you about in the stock market are incredible strategies, but why not do them in a Pension Plan? Why not buy and sell, do the Range Riders, do the Rolling Stock, invest for dividends, do all those incredible strategies that help you get 80, 100, or 200% returns on your money? Do all of these strategies in a Pension Plan, so that you don't get killed on taxes.

USE A VARIETY OF ENTITIES

Use a variety of these different entities. For example, you can have a Keogh plan, but if you have a Keogh plan then you do not qualify for a SEP-IRA. You can have an IRA and you can put aside the $2,000 into an IRA. I've helped people, for example, set up a corporate Pension Plan for one of their businesses, but they had another business that was a partnership with their children. They set up a plan there, and they're putting aside money for their children in the partnership plan. Use these different types of retirement accounts to have your investments in-that's diversity.

The next thing is that you need to diversify your investments. You need to get involved in a variety of different things. Now, please understand that I really believe that the Pension Plan should have a mission, it should have a theme, it should have a central area that it focuses on.

For example, if you're going to get good at Rolling Stock, then have your Pension Plan buy and sell those three or four stocks that you're really good at. If you're going to do mutual funds, get really good at mutual funds. Study them. A Pension Plan should have a theme, but while it has a lot of its money tied up in one central type of investment, it can also get involved in things like limited partnership units in some real estate investments or other kinds of debt. It can buy bonds. By the way, a perfect type of investment would be the zero coupon bond. Remember that one with the phantom income? Well, you don't have to worry about phantom income in the Pension Plan, because it pays no taxes. Why not then in an IRA or in a corporate Pension Plan, buy that zero coupon bond that will mature when you're 65, and a big one to mature when you're 70? Hey, you want to have a huge good time and travel the world when you're 70. So buy a bunch of bonds today that will mature when you're 70, and then you pull them out of the Pension Plan at that point in time.

I could just spend whole days talking about the flexibility, the freedom and the power it brings you when you understand about investing in an entity that pays no taxes. Everything else you're doing, if you get rich under your name, every April 15th you have to pay taxes to the IRS. If you get rich under a corporation, it has to pay taxes. The Pension Plan just sits there and waves at the IRS on April 15th. So, that's the entity that you should use.

LIMITED PARTNERSHIPS

Let me show you how to gift away assets. If you have stock in a corporation, you can just start gifting away the stock. If you have units or stock in a trust, you can start gifting that away also. But the entity that I'd like to share with you right now is a limited partnership. We're going to call it a Family Limited Partnership, because a lot of times people only involve their families in it.

The word limited means limited liability—if ten investors put in $10,000 to form a partnership to buy an apartment complex, they have $100,000. Let's say I'm the general partner and I take the investors' $100,000 and invest it. Now, let's say I forget to get insurance on it, the place burns down and we lose everything. What could you lose? You're limited in your liability; you can lose your $10,000. What about me? I can lose everything, I'm the general partner. I have general liability. They could put liens on my house, I could lose my business, I could lose everything.

When I see a man setting up a limited partnership my hat goes off to him. By the way, I'm the least chauvinistic guy you'll ever meet. Why did I say "man" there? I've been reviewing limited partnerships for over 17 years now. I've reviewed over 300 limited partnerships, and to this day not one time have I seen a woman be the general partner. Not one time. Now why is that? Well, I think they're too smart. I think that women realize that if they're going to put their necks on the line and risk losing everything, they're not going to get involved.

Well, I just bad mouthed being the general partner, but you still need to be the general partner. Male or female, you need to be the general partner. Simply put, you control the checkbook. You need to have the checkbook for this partnership, so you can control the direction of the investments and the direction of the company.

Limited partnerships can run businesses, they can have investments, they have their own federal ID number, they can have a brokerage account—they are separate legal entities. I like limited partnerships; I like them almost as much as corporations. A limited partnership can't have an off year-end like a corporation can have, but they're still limited in liability, just like a corporation is. The tax consequences of limited partnerships are really exciting—a limited partnership pays no taxes in and of itself.

Say that at the end of the year you own 5% of a partnership, your wife owns 5%, one of your kids owns 17%, another one owns 33%, and you have even given 20% to your mother and your father who are in their 60s or 70s. You gift out all these units. At the end of the year, if this partnership has made $100,000 in profits, the money is taxed down to the limited partners by their respective share of ownership. There are no taxes at the partnership level. (By the way, when we set up a limited partnership for people, we set it up with 100,000 units, and the units are then divvied up among the different people by percentages.)

Don't get me wrong, you don't have to actually give your money to the kids; your kids never see a dime of this money. It's just allocated to them in their tax brackets, and the money just goes into your own household checking account. You're buying groceries with it; you're going to the movies with it—the partnership is not taxed. It fills out an information return, a Form 1065, but the money is taxed down to the individual partners.

Let's say that you currently are worth a lot of money. You could set up a limited partnership for running a business; it has no assets of its own. It's a cash flow entity. It runs a business, it has a business, or it manages another business, and it just receives money and distributes money. That's one way of getting money into different tax brackets. But, let's say that you do have some existing assets: $600,000, $1 million, maybe even $2 million.

First of all, I really believe that if you're worth $2 to $3 million you should have multiple corporations. I don't think any one entity should own over 20% of all of your investments. So you should have at least five different legal entities.

For example, if you are worth $1 million, you should have three corporations and two limited partnerships that have about $200,000 equity in each of them. You could also set up a fourth corporation. If you have a lot of equity in another corporation or a lot of equity in your personal residence, with a corporation or a limited partnership you could put a deed of trust or a mortgage against your own personal residence. You could encumber all of the equity in your house, so if anybody ever sues you, they can never get at any of the equity. You do that as a trade.

You trade stock in a corporation and you give it to your kids or your grandkids. Then you put a lien against the property in the name of the corporation and you record the deed so that you can never ever lose the equity in your property.

Let's take a little time out here, we'll get back to the partnership in just a second. My job at the Wealth Academy, and my job as I go through this consulting series with a lot of people is to make them totally invincible. I literally set up a financial fortress around them so that they'll never lose anything. They could grow and become worth hundreds of thousands of dollars, but they'll never ever lose anything.

Now, let's get back to the partnership and I'll show you what that means from a couple of different angles. I'm going to use this example. You take your $2 million and put it into several partnerships. You deed, you assign, you transfer $2 million into the partnership. Now the units are divided. If you do it this way and you own everything, all the investments in the partnership, in this example the 100,000 units probably would have been 50,000 to mom and 50,000 to dad when the partnership was first set up. Now, think this one through, these are units. You have a ledger in the back of your partnership book and you have 100,000 units, 50,000 to mom, 50,000 to dad. Can mom now give some of her units away? Figure out how much her units are worth and she can give them all away, but with no tax consequences.

She could give away $10,000 a year in these units. So she takes $10,000 and deeds them, assigns them to her children. Every year she gives away $10,000. You see what we've just done? We've now set up an entity that allows you to take control of your investments outside of your personal name, have the units owned by the mom and the dad, and then gift them away to the kids. Mom and dad are still the general partners.

They should keep 1% of the partnership units no matter what, but they could gift away 98 or 99% of all the units to their children, to their grandchildren, to their own mom and dad. They could give away everything, and still control the whole investment. They draw out all the salaries, they decide how much is going into Pension Plans, they have full control.

Now, let's see if we've solved the problem of gifting. The gifting problem was that you don't have a grouping of assets. Well, that problem is gone, because now you have nice, neat little groups of assets that you can give away.

When all the gifting is completed you still want to live that big happy life, you still control all the money in the partnership. See, the partnership now owns the investments, owns the rental properties, owns your businesses, et cetera. By the way, just to avoid personal liability, when you set it up make sure that your Nevada Corporation is the general partner. So your corporation, not you personally, is the general partner. This gives you another way of moving money out of your state to Nevada, and a bank account there to lessen your taxes, and you've avoided all personal liability

CHARITABLE REMAINDER TRUSTS

I very seldom get excited about a legal entity like I have about the Charitable Remainder Trust. This is a phenomenal entity with a little twist to it that makes it really exciting. There are four kinds of trusts. Most of them don't work for what I'm going to show you.

What I'm talking about is a Charitable Remainder Unitrust. Let's say you're making $50,000 a year, and you've got some investments, some rental properties, and all that. You can set up a trust, what is called a charitable remainder unitrust—technically, it's called a split interest trust.

The split interest in this trust is going to be this: you will be the income beneficiary and you'll choose a charity to get the investments that you place into the trust when you die. That will be the charity beneficiary. This charity beneficiary could be your church—I recommend that, because you have 30 and 50% charities. The government has an approved list of 50% charities, and churches fall into that category. You donate to this charity some appreciated stock or real estate. You're the trustee of this trust, you control all the investments held in trust, which could have been a rental property or anything else. You sell that property for cash.

The point is that you now get a $100,000 donation. You get a deduction. If it's a 50% charity that's eventually going to get the money, then you can deduct 50% of your current income. Well, if you're making $50,000 a year you get a $25,000 donation deduction, and now your income is only $25,000. If you're making $180,000 you could take $90,000 off and not pay taxes on that. Think about what I just said: you've been able to take something and give it to a charity that you really like, that you want to have the money later on, but you get a deduction right now, and an incredible savings off your income tax.

Now, if you take a $25,000 deduction this year, and you donated a $100,000 asset, you still have $75,000. So you take 50% of your income next year, then 50% the next year, and so on until that $100,000 is gone. Later on you could even donate something else. You can continue to make donations to this charity.

Now, each year, because you're the income beneficiary, you have to pull out 5%, even up to 15%, but you have to take out at least 5% of the assets. So, if you have $100,000 in there, you need to pull out $5,000. But hold it, we're going to show you a real neat angle to this.

If you use us to set up your CRT—Charitable Remainder Trust—we'll set it up with what is called "makeup provisions." What this means is that if you cannot pull out the money, if there's no income in the trust now, you'll be able to make that income when those assets eventually make money. So you have this makeup provision in the trust.

Now you take the $100,000 and buy stock with it, but you don't have that stock make dividends. So, year after year they're growing in value but they don't produce any dividends. Later on, when you're 65 years old, let's say that you have $400,000 in this trust. Your income is going to go down substantially. You know, you have a little Social Security, a Pension Plan, and your income will go down from $80,000 or $90,000 a year; to around $45,000 a year. But now, remember, you've got this $400,000 sitting there.

You have to pull out 5% of it, but here's what you do: at the age of 62 or 65 you start changing all the kinds of investments. Because it's time to retire, now you start buying high income investments, high yielding investments. You switch off the high growth to high yields. Well, it's easy to get 10% from them, a lot of mutual funds get 14 to 15%, but you get 10%. Well, 5% of $400,000 at that time is $20,000. You have to pull that out. But remember your return, 10% of the $400,000 is $40,000.

You've got $400,000 in investments in this account that you're the trustee of; 10% of that is $40,000. You pull out 5% of the $400,000, or $20,000. Remember all that money you didn't pull out for the last 20 to 30 years because there was no income in the trust? Well, with that makeup provision you start to pull out that money, or the balance of this $40,000, or another $20,000.

Let's say at the age of retirement you're making $60,000 a year. Your Pension Plan and Social Security takes your income down to $25,000; however, now you have $20,000 coming out and another $20,000, you're now at $65,000 a year and it's time to live the good life.

You've now lessened your estate. If you put all these donations into the charity, based on what they could have been worth in your own estate, your family would have to pay estate taxes on that. However, you've donated them to the Charitable Remainder Trust, and it's outside of your estate right now because this is a grantor trust, and you can't get the assets back out. By the way, the trust could also pay the premiums on a life insurance policy through an irrevocable life insurance trust. It could do that. It could pay all of the entities. You'll have to claim that premium as income, but now you ask, "What about my kids?"

First of all, this should not have been your only entity. You should still have a Living Trust and other entities to take care of your family. This one is for the excess things that you want to go to a charity upon your death. You buy a second life insurance policy on your husband or wife because the trust is going to stay in existence until the second person dies. Upon the death of the second spouse, husband or wife, the trust or the life insurance pays off $400,000 to your kids. They get everything that they were going to get anyway, and still the charity gets the other $400,000 in investments at that point in time. What a neat thing that you can do. You take deductions now, lessen your estate now, make sure your kids are taken care of, profit by incredible cash flow for yourself either now and/or in the future. This CRT is a phenomenal way to go.

INTEGRATING YOUR ENTITIES

This strategy is about the integration of all of these entities. There are three basic entities, and five total that I really think are important here in the United States. The three basic entities are the corporation, the Living Trust, and the Pension Plan. Those are the three basic entities that everybody needs. The other entities that you can pick and choose from are the Limited Partnership and the Charitable Remainder Trust. Now you understand these entities and how they work together.

For example, the corporation can be the general partner of the partnership. A partnership can own stock in a corporation. The stock that you also own in a corporation could and should be owned by your Living Trust, in order to make sure that none of the stock is in your own name.

You could take one corporation and put liens against your other corporation, or put liens against your personal residence to avoid any threat of lawsuits, and even if you do get sued you won't lose any of your equity. You can integrate these entities in so many ways that there's just no way that I can do justice to all of them in this book.

When you let us set up your entities we literally sit there with you and custom design them—have your corporation here, that moves money over here; that corporation does this and this; your Living Trust up here is an umbrella entity and owns the stock in this; you have your personal residence here, this is what you do here; you move money into a Pension Plan over here. It is really, really fun to show people how to integrate these entities.

I also have a good video tape of this, that is part of a bonus included with the Financial Fortress set of books and tapes. It's called the Entity Integration Video. It's about an hour and a half of me actually designing and diagramming these different entities, as you watch. I encourage you to sit down and take time to structure yourself, and to learn how these different entities interact with each other.

TAKING CARE OF YOU

Take care of "You"—nobody is going to do this for you. You imagine tonight your CPA getting home, snuggling down into bed, pulling his covers up around his neck, and you tell me how much he's worried about your financial situation. You need to set these things up and do them yourself. You need to get going. You need to not only understand these different entities but you need to set them up. I have prototype Living Trust documents available to help you.

I'm amazed at how many people buy our prototype Living Trust documents and go home and do nothing about it. Literally tens of thousands of dollars of information is in those documents, and some people don't even use them. Well, it's time to get going. It's time to quit making excuses and get these entities set up, so that you are financially fit for opportunity—if you don't do it nobody else will. So, you've got to get the information and you've got to get these entities set up. If my company can be of help in doing that, can help you get these things structured so that you are financially fit so you can sleep when the wind blows, then great. I'd love to help you do that.

III AVAILABLE RESOURCES

The following books, videos, and audiocassettes have been reviewed by the Wade Cook Seminars, Inc. or Lighthouse Publishing Group, Inc. staff and are suggested as reading and resource material for continuing education to help with your financial planning, and real estate and stock market investments. Because new ideas and techniques come along and laws change, we're always updating our catalog.

To order a copy of our current catalog, please write or call us at:

Wade Cook Seminars, Inc.
14675 Interurban Avenue South
Seattle, Washington 98168-4664
1-800-872-7411

Or, visit us on our web sites at:
www.wadecook.com
www.lighthousebooks.com

Also, we would love to hear your comments on our products and services, as well as your testimonials on how these products have benefited you. We look forward to hearing from you!

AUDIOCASSETTES

INCOME FORMULAS-A FREE CASSETTE

By Wade B. Cook

Learn the 11 cash flow formulas taught in the Wall Street Workshop. Learn to double some of your money in 2 $1/2$ to 4 months.

ZERO TO ZILLIONS

By Wade B. Cook

This is a powerful audio workshop on Wall Street-understanding the stock market game, playing it successfully, and retiring rich. Learn 11 powerful investment strategies to avoid pitfalls and losses, catch "Day-trippers," "Bottom fish," write Covered Calls, options on stock split companies, and so much more. Wade "Meter Drop" Cook will teach you how he makes fantastic annual returns in your account.

POWER OF NEVADA CORPORATIONS-A FREE CASSETTE

By Wade B. Cook

Nevada Corporations have secrecy, privacy, minimal taxes, no reciprocity with the IRS, and protection for shareholders, officers, and directors. This is a powerful seminar.

INCOME STREAMS-A FREE CASSETTE

By Wade B. Cook

Learn to buy and sell real estate the Wade Cook way. This informative cassette will instruct you in building and operating your own real estate money machine.

MONEY MACHINE I & II

By Wade B. Cook

Learn the benefits of buying, and more importantly, selling real estate. Now the system for creating and maintaining a real

---

estate money machine is available in audiocassette form. Money Machine I & II teach the step by step cash flow formulas that made Wade Cook and thousands like him millions of dollars.

MONEY MYSTERIES OF THE MILLIONAIRES
A FREE CASSETTE

By Wade B. Cook

How to make money and keep it. This fantastic seminar shows you how to use Nevada Corporations, Living Trusts, Pension Plans, Charitable Remainder Trusts, and Family Limited Partnerships to protect your assets.

UNLIMITED WEALTH AUDIO SET

By Wade B. Cook

Unlimited Wealth is the "University of Money-Making Ideas" home study course that helps you improve your money's personality. The heart and soul of this seminar is to make more money, pay fewer taxes, and keep more for your retirement and family. This cassette series contains the great ideas from Wealth 101 on tape, so you can listen to them whenever you want.

RETIREMENT PROSPERITY

By Wade B. Cook

Take that IRA money now sitting idle and invest it in ways that generate you bigger, better, and quicker returns. This four audiotape set walks you through a system of using a self directed IRA to create phenomenal profits, virtually tax free! This is one of the most complete systems for IRA investing ever created.

THE FINANCIAL FORTRESS HOME STUDY COURSE

By Wade B. Cook

This eight-part series is the last word in entity structuring. It goes far beyond mere financial planning or estate planning. It helps you structure your business and your affairs so that you can avoid the majority of taxes, retire rich, escape lawsuits, bequeath your assets to your heirs without government interference, and, in short-bomb proof your entire estate. There are six audio cassette seminars on tape, an entity structuring video, and a full kit of documents.

PAPER TIGERS AND PAPER CHASE

By Wade B. Cook

Wade gives you a personal introduction to the art of buying and selling real estate. In this set of six cassettes, Wade shares his inside secrets to establishing a cash flow business with real estate investments. You will learn how to find discounted second mortgages, find second mortgage notes and make them better, as well as how you can get 40%-plus yields on your money. Learn the art of structuring your business to attract investors and bring in the income you desire through the use of family corporations, pension plans, and other legal entities. A manual is included.

When you buy Paper Tigers, you'll also receive Paper Chase for free. Paper Chase holds the most important tools you need to make deals happen. Wade created these powerful tapes as a hand-out tool you can lend to potential investors or home owners to help educate them about how this amazing cash flow system works for them. It explains how you'll negotiate a lower interest rate if they make a larger payment. You will use this incredible tool over and over again.

BOOKS IN BOOKSTORES

WALL STREET MONEY MACHINE

By Wade B. Cook

Appearing on the New York Times Business Best Sellers list for over one year, **Wall Street Money Machine** contains the best strategies for wealth enhancement and cash flow creation you'll find anywhere. Throughout this book, Wade Cook describes many of his favorite strategies for generating cash flow through the stock market: Rolling Stock, Proxy Investing, Covered Calls, and many more. It's a great introduction for creating wealth using the Wade Cook formulas.

STOCK MARKET MIRACLES

By Wade B. Cook

The anxiously-awaited partner to *Wall Street Money Machine*, this book is proven to be just as invaluable. *Stock Market Miracles* improves on some of the strategies from *Wall Street Money Machine*, as well as introduces new and valuable twists on our old favorites. This is a must read for anyone interested in making serious money in the stock market.

BEAR MARKET BALONEY

By Wade B. Cook

A more timely book wouldn't be possible. Wade's predictions came true while the book was at press! Don't miss this insightful look into what makes bull and bear markets and how to make exponential returns in any market.

REAL ESTATE MONEY MACHINE

By Wade B. Cook

Wade's first bestselling book reveals the secrets of Wade Cook's own system-the system he earned his first million from. This book teaches you how to make money regardless of the state of the economy. Wade's innovative concepts for investing in real estate not only avoids high interest rates, but avoids banks altogether.

HOW TO PICK UP FORECLOSURES

By Wade B. Cook

Do you want to become an expert money maker in real estate? This book will show you how to buy real estate at 60¢ on the dollar or less. You'll learn to find the house before the auction and purchase it with no bank financing-the easy way to millions in real estate. The market for foreclosures is a tremendous place to learn and prosper. *How To Pick Up Foreclosures* takes Wade's methods from *Real Estate Money Machine* and super charges them by applying the fantastic principles to already-discounted properties.

OWNER FINANCING

By Wade B. Cook

This is a short but invaluable booklet you can give to sellers who hesitate to sell you their property using the owner financing method. Let this pamphlet convince both you and them. The special report, *"Why Sellers Should Take Monthly Payments,"* is included for free!

REAL ESTATE FOR REAL PEOPLE

By Wade B. Cook

A priceless, comprehensive overview of real estate investing, this book teaches you how to buy the right property for the right price, at the right time. Wade Cook explains all of the strategies you'll need, and gives you 20 reasons why you should start investing in real estate today. Learn how to retire rich with real estate, and have fun doing it.

101 WAYS TO BUY REAL ESTATE WITHOUT CASH

By Wade B. Cook

Wade Cook has personally achieved success after success in real estate. *101 Ways To Buy Real Estate Without Cash* fills the gap left by other authors who have given all the ingredients but not the whole recipe for real estate investing. This is the book for the investor who wants innovative and practical methods for buying real estate with little or no money down.

BLUEPRINTS FOR SUCCESS, VOLUME 1

Contributors: Wade Cook, Debbie Losse, Joel Black, Dan Wagner, Tim Semingson, Rich Simmons, Greg Witt, JJ Childers, Keven Hart, Dave Wagner and Steve Wirrick

Blueprints for Success, Volume 1 is a compilation of chapters on building your wealth through your business and making your business function successfully. The chapters cover: education and information gathering, choosing the best business for you from all the different types of business, and a variety of other skills necessary for becoming successful. Your business can't afford to miss out on these powerful insights!

BRILLIANT DEDUCTIONS

By Wade B. Cook

Do you want to make the most of the money you earn? Do you want to have solid tax havens and ways to reduce the taxes you pay? This book is for you! Learn how to get rich in spite of the updated 1997 tax laws. See new tax credits, year-end maneuvers, and methods for transferring and controlling your entities. Learn to structure yourself and your family for tax savings and liability protection. Available in bookstores or call our toll free number: 1-800-872-7411.

WEALTH 101

By Wade B. Cook

This incredible book brings you 101 strategies for wealth creation and protection that you can't afford to miss. Front to back, it is packed full of tips and tricks to supercharge your financial health. If you need to generate more cash flow, this book shows you how through several various avenues. If you are already wealthy, this is the book that will show you strategy upon strategy for decreasing your tax liability and increasing your peace of mind through liability protection.

WADE COOK'S POWER QUOTES

By Wade B. Cook

This book is a collection of the best wisdom for every area of life. If you want to succeed, you cannot afford to miss this incredible opportunity to have the advice of some of the most successful minds who have ever lived. Make a point to start every day with a burst of wisdom to help guide you through life's obstacles.

VIDEOS

DYNAMIC DOLLARS VIDEO

By Wade B. Cook

Wade Cook's 90 minute introduction to the basics of his Wall Street formulas and strategies. In this presentation, designed especially for video, Wade explains the meter drop philosophy, Rolling Stock, basics of Proxy Investing, and writing Covered Calls. Perfect for anyone looking for a little basic information.

THE WALL STREET WORKSHOP VIDEO SERIES
By Wade B. Cook

If you can't make it to the Wall Street Workshop soon, get a head start with these videos. Ten albums containing 11 hours of intense instruction on Rolling Stock, options on stock split companies, writing Covered Calls, and eight other tested and proven strategies designed to help you increase the value of your investments. By learning, reviewing, and implementing the strategies taught here, you will gain the knowledge and the confidence to take control of your investments, and get your money to work hard for you.

THE NEXT STEP VIDEO SERIES
By Team Wall Street

The advanced version of the Wall Street Workshop. Full of power-packed strategies from Wade Cook, this is not a duplicate of the Wall Street Workshop, but a very important partner. The methods taught in this seminar will supercharge the strategies taught in the Wall Street Workshop and teach you even more ways to make more money!

In The Next Step, you'll learn how to find the stocks to fit the formulas through technical analysis, fundamentals, home trading tools, and more.

BUILD PERPETUAL INCOME (BPI)-A VIDEOCASSETTE

Wade Cook Seminars, Inc. is proud to present Build Perpetual Income, the latest in our ever-expanding series of seminar home study courses. In this video, you will learn powerful real estate cash-flow generating techniques, such as:

- Power negotiating strategies
- Buying and selling mortgages
- Writing contracts
- Finding and buying discount properties
- Avoiding debt

CLASSES OFFERED

COOK UNIVERSITY

The backbone of the one-year Cook University program is the Money Machine concept-as applied to your business, to stock investments, or to real estate. Although there are many, many other forms of investing in real estate, there are really only three that work: the Money Machine method, buying second mortgages, and lease options. Of these three, the Money Machine stands head and shoulders above the rest.

It is difficult to explain Cook University in only a few words. It is so unique, innovative and creative that it literally stands alone. But then, what would you expect from Wade Cook? Something common and ordinary? Never! Wade and his staff always go out of their way to provide you with useful, tried-and-true strategies that create real wealth.

Cook University is designed to be an integral part of your educational life. We encourage you to call and find out more about this life-changing program. The number is 1-800-872-7411. Ask for an enrollment director and begin your millionaire-training today!

If you want to be wealthy, this is the place to be.

THE WALL STREET WORKSHOP

Presented by Wade B. Cook and Team Wall Street

The Wall Street Workshop teaches you how to make incredible money in all markets. It teaches you the tried-and-true strategies that have made hundreds of people wealthy.

THE NEXT STEP WORKSHOP

Presented by Wade B. Cook and Team Wall Street

An Advanced Wall Street Workshop designed to help those ready to take their trading to the next level and treat it as a business. This seminar is open only to graduates of the Wall Street Workshop.

EXECUTIVE RETREAT

Presented by Wade B. Cook and Team Wall Street

Created especially for the individuals already owning or planning to establish Nevada Corporations, the Executive Retreat is a unique opportunity for corporate executives to participate in workshops geared toward streamlining operations and maximizing efficiency and impact.

WEALTH INSTITUTE

Presented by Wade B. Cook and Team Wall Street

This three day workshop defines the art of asset protection and entity planning. During these three days we will discuss, in depth and detail, the six domestic entities that will protect you from lawsuits, taxes, or other financial losses, and help you retire rich.

REAL ESTATE WORKSHOP

Presented by Wade B. Cook and Team Main Street

The Real Estate Workshop teaches you how to build perpetual income for life, without going to work. Some of the topics include buying and selling paper, finding discounted properties, generating long-term monthly cash flow, and controlling properties without owning them.

REAL ESTATE BOOTCAMP

Presented by Wade B. Cook and Team Main Street

This three to four day Bootcamp is truly a roll-up-your-sleeves-and-do-the-deals event. You will be learning how to locate the bargains, negotiate strategies, and find wholesale properties (pre-foreclosures). You will also visit a title company, look at properties and learn some new and fun selling strategies.

BUSINESS ENTITY SKILLS TRAINING (BEST)

Presented by Wade B. Cook and Team Wall Street

Learn about the six powerful entities you can use to protect your wealth and your family. Learn the secrets of asset protection, eliminate your fear of litigation, and minimize your taxes.

ASSORTED RESOURCES

WEALTH INFORMATION NETWORK (WIN)

This subscription internet service provides you with the latest financial formulas and updated entity structuring strategies. New, timely information is entered Monday through Friday, sometimes four or five times a day. Wade Cook and his Team Wall Street staff write for WIN, giving you updates on their own current stock plays, companies who announced earnings, companies who announced stock splits, and the latest trends in the market.

WIN is also divided into categories according to specific strategies and contains archives of all our trades so you can view our history. If you are just getting started in the stock market, this is a great way to follow people who are doubling some of their money every $2^1/2$ to 4 months. If you are experienced already, it's the way to confirm your feelings and research with others who are generating wealth through the stock market. (www.wadecook.com)

IQ PAGER

This is a system that beeps you as events and announcements are made on Wall Street. With IQ Pager, you'll receive information about events like major stock split announcements, earnings surprises, important mergers and acquisitions, judgements or court decisions involving big companies, important bankruptcy announcements, big winners and losers, and disasters. The key to the stock market is timing. Especially when you're trading in options, you need up-to-the-minute (or second) information. You cannot afford to sit at a computer all day looking for news or wait for your broker to call. The IQ Pager is the ideal partner to the Wealth Information Network (WIN).

THE INCORPORATION HANDBOOK

By Wade B. Cook

Incorporation made easy! This handbook tells you who, why, and, most importantly, how to incorporate. Included are samples of the forms you will use when you incorporate, as well as a step-by-step guide from the experts.

LEGAL FORMS

By Wade B. Cook

This collection of pertinent forms contains numerous legal forms used in real estate transactions. These forms were selected by experienced investors, but are not intended to replace the advice of an attorney. However, they will provide essential forms for you to follow in your personal investing.

RECORD KEEPING SYSTEM

By Wade B. Cook

A complete record keeping system for organizing all of the information on each of your properties. This system keeps track of everything from insurance policies to equity growth. You will know at a glance exactly where you stand with your investment properties and you will sleep better at night.

TRAVEL AGENT INFORMATION

By John Childers and Wade Cook

The only sensible solution for the frequent traveler. This kit includes all of the information and training you need to be an outside travel agent for a stable company. There are no hassles, no requirements, no forms or restrictions, just all the benefits of traveling for substantially less every time. For additional information and pricing call 1-800-872-7411.

JUST RELEASED!

24 KARAT SEMINAR ON CASSETTE

By Wade Cook

Learn how to protect your family's finances through any disaster—including Y2K! The 24 Karat seminar on cassette teaches people how to hedge against inflation, prepare for catastrophe, and invest in the safest currency. This seminar is packed with must-know information about your future.